PSYWARRIORS

Psychological Warfare during the Korean War

By

Alan K. Abner

BURD STREET PRESS
SHIPPENSBURG, PENNSYLVANIA

This Burd Street Press publication
was printed by
Beidel Printing House, Inc.
63 West Burd Street
Shippensburg, PA 17257-0152 USA

In respect for the scholarship contained herein, the acid-free paper used in this book meets the guidelines for permanence and durability of the Committee on Production Guidelines for Book Longevity of the Council on Library Resources.

For a complete list of available publications
please write
Burd Street Press
Division of White Mane Publishing Company, Inc.
P.O. Box 152
Shippensburg, PA 17257-0152 USA

Library of Congress Cataloging-in-Publication Data

Abner, Alan K., 1921-
    Psywarriors : pychological warfare during the Korean War / by Alan K. Abner.
        p. cm.
    ISBN 1-57249-233-3 (alk. paper)
    1. Korean War, 1950-1953--Psychological aspects. 2. Psychological warfare--Korea. I. Title.

DS921.5.P78 A26 2000
951.904'2--dc21

                                                                    00-064244

Dedication
To Donna Kinney Abner:
Copilot, navigator, crew-chief.

Contents

Preface vi

Chapter I   Police Action 1

Chapter II   Trust Truman? 6

Chapter III   Flashback 11

Chapter IV   Call to Arms 19

Chapter V   Flying Time 28

Chapter VI   Class Action 32

Chapter VII   Georgetown University 39

Chapter VIII   Secret Witness 44

Chapter IX   Propaganda 50

Chapter X   Think Tank 58

Chapter XI $10,000 Mig 71

Chapter XII   "Big Mac" 77

Chapter XIII   This Is the Army 81

Chapter XIV   "The Directors" 91

Chapter XV   Ed Murrow 99

Chapter XVI   Miami Mission 106

Chapter XVII   "Over and Out" 113

Epilogue 118

Preface

Psywarriors is a narrative account by a WWII fighter pilot, who after a brief four-year respite from combat was recalled in 1950 to active duty during the Korean War to again serve his country. This time, not to engage an enemy in the skies of Europe, but to wage a war of words against the Soviet Union and its proxy military forces in Korea. Captain Alan K. Abner was charged with the direction of an elite cadre of "the cream of the crop" of 1951 college honor graduates who became the first United States Air Force psywarriors.

The announcement of the war presented difficulties not only to the military in the battle zone, but also created widespread disappointment and apprehension of those veterans of WWII who were still engaged in a private conflict adjusting to civilian life. It was a period of old memories, and a time of new challenges.

Chapter I

Police Action

"What's this 'Police Action' in Korea crap? It's another goddamn war, that's what it is!" This expression in various forms was heard in VFW (Veterans of Foreign Wars), American Legion Chapters, bars and taverns, and more politely from platforms and pulpits across the nation. The now dwindling numbers of veterans from WWI, "The war to end all wars," shook their graying heads in disbelief. The thousands of those who had worn their combat gear during WWII on the high seas, in the air, in the mud of the Ardennes or the jungles of the South Pacific shook their fists in frustration.

What is a "Police Action"? First of all, it's a more palatable term for war. It was a label adopted by President Truman's word-smiths, the same folks that came up with "Give 'em hell, Harry." This reasonable sounding term enabled their leader to make it easier for Congress to approve his action, and to persuade the United Nations to cautiously endorse and support the United States intervention in this Asian peninsula. It worked. There was no declaration of war, and no one liked that historic phrase. But there was little doubt in the minds of nearly everyone that the brief peacetime honeymoon was over.

My usual Sunday night phone call brought a minor explosion from my dad. "What in tarnation is a police action?" I was really surprised at his reaction to the news. He was a lifelong Jeffersonian Democrat and he rarely was at odds with our presidents, Roosevelt and Truman alike. I could only recall a couple of incidents when he had disagreed; when FDR had tried to "pack" the Supreme Court,

and Truman when he persisted in maintaining his outspoken loyalty to Tom Pendergrast, the infamous Kansas City political boss.

He didn't immediately condemn the police action, but as the
news coverage unfolded and troop movements were announced, he
too called it a war. And he wasn't confused as to who was the enemy. "It was those damned Ruskies!"

Japan, August 6, 1945, at 8:15 A.M. marked the beginning of the
atomic age with the bombing of Hiroshima. Three days later Nagasaki
was destroyed by a second attack.

Although Truman made the final decision to use the atomic
weapon he first sought the advice of his military advisors. General
George Marshall at first opposed its use but later yielded to the unani-
mous endorsements of Admiral Ernest King, General Eisenhower,
Admiral William D. Leahy and 90 percent of 150 American scientists
polled earlier who approved use of the bomb.

Earlier on July 26 the U.S. government issued an ultimatum to
Japan to surrender and dropped 27 million leaflets warning of the
consequences if they did not. Now with two cities almost completely
obliterated, Japan surrendered August 4. V.J. Day was declared September 2, 1945, ending WWII.

America's action was estimated to have saved the lives of
500,000 American soldiers, sailors, marines, and airmen.

I recall this historic moment clearly. My comrades and I in the
357th Fighter Group were poised in Munich, Germany, awaiting orders to proceed to the Japanese Theater to join the battle. When the
news broke, we celebrated! Though "Give 'em hell, Harry" had a
new and sobering significance.

* * * * *

My commander in chief, Franklin D. Roosevelt, died April 11,
1945. I was flying combat with the 357th Fighter Group in England.
Roosevelt was the only president most of my comrades and I had
ever really known. And like most of my mates, I had to pause to
remember the name of Harry Truman, his successor.

The next letter from home was somewhat reassuring. Obviously my dad had been following Truman's career as vice president with more than casual interest. I recall the gist of some of his comments about our new commander in chief.

Truman first became generally known nationally as the author and chairman of the Senate War Investigative Committee in 1941 that was designed to halt the graft and exploitation that was merging in the war production business similar to the scandalous activities by profiteers in WWI. In the summer of 1943 Truman claimed, and it was confirmed, that his investigators had saved the country 15 billion dollars at a cost of 400,000 dollars. And, by the start of 1944 he was being touted as a possible candidate for the second spot on FDR's upcoming election ticket. At the Democrat National Convention he beat out a challenge by Henry Wallace on the second ballot. He only needed 192 words for his acceptance speech.

My dad offered a couple of human interest sidebars. He said that Truman had seen active duty in WWI as a captain and artillery company commander and had seen some rough combat in France. Unlike some of the more "hawkish" members of Congress, he would not be eager to risk the lives of American soldiers in a military adventure. Furthermore, he added tongue in cheek, Truman had been a farmer (like my dad), and at one time a clothing store owner (also like Roy Abner) . . . "you know, Harry has to be a pretty regular follow."

I do not remember my dad ever referring to FDR in any way other than President Roosevelt. I was intrigued and in a strange way reassured that he thought of President Truman as "Harry."

* * * * *

Early in June 1947, after a few months of adjustment to civilian life, I finally hung my white silk scarf and my leather A-2 jacket, emblazoned with the logo of the 357th Fighter Group, in the closet and put on a quite handsome tweed suit, a bow tie, and became a radio newsman.

There was, of course, considerably more to this career change than haberdashery, but I soon became reasonably competent and joined a small-market radio station as a reporter, editor, on-the-air anchor . . . you name it.

My daily chores included covering city council meetings, county commission sessions, fires, murders, wakes, and weddings, but also much to my satisfaction, I was required to follow the local news with national releases provided by United Press International news wire service. UPI also provided a continuous flow of commentary, analysis, sports, stock market profiles, and a variety of features. Locally, I also had the opportunity to interview visiting dignitaries which we carried "live" before the days of tape recorders. But the highlight of all visits by VIPs was the 1948 Whistle Stop re-election campaign of President Harry Truman.

I must say as a waffling "Republicrat" that I had become a fan of Harry Truman. And as the news editor of KFJI Radio, Klamath Falls, Oregon, I ordered a Class A telephone line from the Southern Pacific Railroad station to our studio on Main Street and prepared to cover his visit to our city. The morning of the big day Ed Boyd, my technician, checked our "feed" from our broadcast site as the sun was coming up, and we were ready. First to arrive on the scene were a few hundred curious citizens, and a loud mix of loyal Democrats. And we all looked up the track for the anticipated arrival of the first 17-car train that carried the escort preceding the president for security checks, followed by the president's train that pulled his Pullman car called "Magellan." This converted sleeper, a 285,000-pound land-going yacht, contained a lounge, four bedrooms, a dining compartment seating 12, and a bath.

Finally, it arrived, and I perched on the coupling just beneath the brass railing bordering the rear platform of the car, and reaching up held a salt shaker mike alongside the public address system microphone to catch the president's speech to the almost rowdy gathering. His remarks were "off the cuff," and delighted the crowd. He introduced "the Boss," Bess Truman, and daughter Margaret. It was Harry Truman, vintage 1948. The event was highlighted, however, by a bedraggled early morning tavern patron who emerged from his oasis across the street some distance from the scene, but who was clearly heard by the president and the crowd as he cried, "Give 'em hell, Harry."

Chapter II

Trust Truman?

1950 . . . It was important to me now to come to some sort of an accommodation with this new war situation and the possible interruption of my recent civilian status. I, like a number of my friends, also veterans, experienced an early disappointment, indeed some anger, at the president's action, and needed a detailed explanation from our government that this conflict was justified. There was no historic precedent . . . no sinking of the *Maine*; no *Lusitania*; no Pearl Harbor; no significant criminal act that had cost American lives. My own search for satisfaction in the situation was to examine and hopefully renew my faith in my government and my trust in the president.

Harry Truman had served only for 82 days as vice president when he succeeded Roosevelt in 1945. The public opinion polls showed his popularity at an 87 percent level at that time. His survey numbers showed a steady decline to 32 percent by November of 1946. The "moment" that would start his historical record of achievement was in February 1947 when he was informed that Britain would cease its military and economic support of Greece in the face of increasing communist pressures that surrounded that country as well as Turkey.

On March 12, 1947, he asked Congress for $250 million in aid for Greece, and $150 million for Turkey to resist the communist rebels in these countries, as well as to deter the threat of the communist governments of Bulgaria, Albania, and Yugoslavia who had stationed troops along the Greek border. This action served to announce the

Truman Doctrine that declared that the United States would assist other nations to withstand communist pressures. Later that summer General George Marshall, who had replaced Jimmy Byrnes as secretary of state, proclaimed Truman's new foreign policy plan in a speech at Harvard University that would become the operational Marshall Plan. This started a program of economic rehabilitation of western European nations as a bulwark against communism. This plan and Truman's aid request were approved by Congress by a vote of 69 to 17.

* * * * *

The Truman Doctrine and the Marshall Plan were early signs that the new president held no delusions as to the role Stalin and Russia and its satellites intended to pursue in gaining worldwide domination. He recalled Winston Churchill's reference to an "Iron Curtain" in a letter from the prime minister in April of 1945, and he was to arrive at a similar conclusion at his first meeting with the Big Three—The United States, England, and Russia.

In July 1945, just three months after taking office, Truman sailed for Potsdam, East Germany, for a meeting with Churchill, British Labor Clement Attlee, who was opposing Churchill in upcoming British elections, and Stalin. Although the sessions started in a more or less amiable fashion, Truman was aware of a growing arrogance and thinly veiled antagonism by the Russian ruler.

At one point during a casual exchange with Stalin, he pressed the Russian on the rights of Catholics in Poland. Stalin responded by asking, "How many divisions has the Pope?" The president, who had just learned of a successful atom bomb test at Alamogordo, New Mexico, told both Churchill and Stalin of this development, and both advised him to use it against Japan.

The Potsdam Conference paused in its proceedings to enable Churchill and Attlee to return to Great Britain for the elections, which surprisingly resulted in the defeat of Churchill. During this interim, Truman went to Frankfurt, Germany, to visit the troops awaiting possible assignment to the Japanese Theater, and to consult with the

Supreme Headquarters Allied Expeditionary Forces (SHAEF) Commander General Dwight D. Eisenhower. During his meetings with Eisenhower and his deputy, Lucius Clay, he reviewed the failure of two generals, Lucius Clay and John Dean, at the time of the cease of hostilities in Europe to insure American access to Berlin after the occupation. He learned that they had accepted an *oral pledge* from Russian General Zhukov instead of a written agreement. (This understanding was later denied by the Russians and resulted in the Berlin Airlift.)

The conference resumed on July 30 with Clement Attlee as the new prime minister and met for the final two days of the 13 sessions with few lasting agreements. Stalin affirmed Russia would enter the war against Japan, but it wasn't until *after* V.J. Day that he delivered.

Truman later revealed his impressions of the conference in a letter to his family when he said, "You never saw such pig-headed people as are the Russians. I hope I never have to hold another conference with them."

Upon his return to Washington, Truman was to learn later that Secretary of State James F. Byrnes had signed a five-year agreement in December at the Moscow Conference of Foreign Ministers that formed a joint trusteeship with the USSR that divided Korea into two sectors, with Russia north of the 38th parallel and the United States in the south. Thus was planted the seed for what was now the occurrence of Russia's proxy war against the United Nations and U.S. forces.

* * * * *

Harry Truman's successful Whistle Stop campaign tour that I had covered in Klamath Falls was completed on June 18, 1948, when he returned to Washington. One week later our UPI wire service confirmed the nomination of Thomas Dewey as his Republican opponent. And on that same day came the announcement that Russia had frozen all traffic access from the Western Occupation Zones in Germany to Berlin, which was surrounded by the Russian Zone. Suddenly, 2,400,000 persons were held captive in Berlin.

This began a historic episode that I regarded as one of Truman's finest hours. He initiated and accelerated the Berlin Airlift operation against the advice of almost all of his cabinet and with the exception of General Lucius Clay, now the commander of the Western Occupation Forces, the Joint Chiefs of Staff including General Hoyt Vandenberg, air force head.

All available transport cargo planes in the American European Command, including the Air Transport Command led by General Mathew Turner, soon had aircraft loaded to capacity, landing every three minutes on the beleaguered city that was cut off and surrounded by 300,000 Soviet troops. By May 12, 1949, when the Russians finally capitulated and the blockade was lifted, they had completed 277,000 flights and suffered 78 casualties. General Clay credited Truman with the decision to challenge the Russians and said, "If Harry Truman was running for president of the world, I'd vote for him."

* * * * *

My "research" in reviewing President Truman's now four years in office was certainly not as scholarly as it probably could have been. Much of it was based on fairly accurate recollections of my father and my own recall of events that was somewhat distracted at the time by my preoccupation with enjoying civilian life and my new career. Now, more recently, a more careful perusal of editorials, wire service commentaries, and news analysis programs provided me with a good deal of reassurance as to the rightness of our cause.

I must admit I had no intention of volunteering for active duty. I was more than willing to accept General Douglas MacArthur's assurance that "the troops will be home by Christmas." And then, there's the chance some network executive will hear my staccato reports or newscasts on our 100 watt signal and say, "Now there's a young guy that should be on our network covering the war."

However, another more serious thought that kept intruding on my efforts to rationalize this new wartime climate was the adjustment that I knew would have to be made by all citizens and of course all of those who had seen active military duty. Especially those who had barely survived the million plus casualties suffered in WWII.

I observed many veterans who were still struggling to forget the horrors of combat they had experienced and were fighting another kind of desperate battle trying to perform in a peaceful environment. Would they be called to do it again? To trade in their straw hats, Levis and T-shirts for steel helmets, fatigue uniforms, and combat boots?

My own memories were still vividly clear. And though not haunted by nightmares as I knew others were, I still had no desire to do it again. As the old saying goes, "We've been there and done that."

Chapter III

Flashback

Was it Thomas Wolfe who said you can't go home again? Well, someone said it, but I didn't believe it. Why in hell can't you go home? After V.E. Day of WWII the prospect of surviving and finally returning home became a lot brighter. My outfit moved to Germany en route to Japan and waited for orders to proceed to the Far East. Except for one mission when we moved into Yugoslavia looking for culprits who had shot down one of our C-47s, we were in a standby position awaiting orders to engage the enemy in the Japanese Theater. Harry Truman and the A-Bomb erased that possibility. The war was truly over, and it was then hurry-up-and-wait. Harry Bridges and his longshoremen called a strike in New York harbor, and I sat in a tent in the mud of Le Havre, France, waiting for a berth in anything that would float going west.

The population of this tent city of Le Havre was made up of a couple of thousand Americans from all branches of the army and air corps who also wanted to go home. It rained constantly, and the only diversion was to sleep, eat field kitchen food, try to figure out a way to smuggle an illegal 45 cal. automatic out in your baggage, and wade through the mud to the officers' club as soon as it opened for an anesthetic to kill the pain in your ass.

The *officers' club* was a huge tent with a well-stocked stand-up bar that was at least 50 feet in length. The place was always packed with thirsty customers, and it was a pretty good trick to find an opening in the plank to place and get your order.

This day I entered this hallowed hall about 10 minutes after opening time and 20 minutes later I had pushed, shoved, and elbowed

11

my way through the wall-to-wall patrons to get to the front rank with those waiting for an opening at the bar. It was then I noticed a peculiar situation. To my right, about 30 feet away was a 15-foot gap in the row of men facing the bar. In the middle of this vacant space was the figure of a man hunched over the bar, resting on his elbows, motionless, staring down at his drink. He was big, he was oblivious to anyone around him, and he was ominous.

"I think he's probably a Section VIII, or at least a guy that's flak happy or something," a man next to me said. "At any rate, he's made it clear he doesn't want company."

I stood there for about five minutes until, finally, I said "What the hell" to myself, and moved cautiously to the bar at the far left side of the blank space to his left. I didn't look at him until I got my drink, a double, straight. It was then, after taking a healthy swig, that I decided to steal a glance, ready to bail out if he became unfriendly.

He was a scroungy looking soldier. He was draped in a well-worn, battered tank corps jacket, dirty woolen blanket pants tucked into muddy, laced infantry boots, and a knit helmet liner cap with a captain's bars pinned on the front. It was then I could see his profile. I knew him!

It was Geof' Jones, my quarterback on the Pacific Quakers' football team I'd played on in college some six long years ago. There was no doubt. It was him, though to say he had aged would be an understatement.

I moved to a spot about five or six feet from him, my right foot braced for a quick retreat, and spoke with a heartiness I didn't really feel.

"Hi, Geof'. How're you doin'? It's me. Alan Abner from Newberg. How do we get outa this dump?"

He slowly turned his head and looked at me. His bloodshot eyes glared at first for about a long ten count, and then the glaze faded and a faint glow of recognition emerged.

"Ab'," he said. "The peace-lovin' Quakers." A long pause . . . "Newberg . . . Portland . . . I'm just tryin' to get home."

* * * * *

I've often wondered how Geof' Jones, after endless months in the infantry, fighting on the ground in North Africa, Italy, and finally Germany, made the transition back to peace-time civilian life.

The problem is you go back to the home you remember. You know things have probably changed a little. But still, there's been no material war damage. You've seen a lot of that, and there can't have been any dramatic alterations to the familiar, relatively small things that have emerged from time to time from your memory bank. The visual things . . . the swimming hole shaded from the late afternoon sun; the tin roofed barn sagging with snow; the miniature rainbows flickering amidst the irrigation sprinklers waving over the alfalfa field; the animals . . . dogs, horses, pigs, and deerlike Jersey heifers. Sounds: tinkling cow bells; the whirr of a pheasant surprised in the brush; the rippling rhythm of the trout stream tumbling over mossy rocks; a far off train whistle. Smells: newly mown hay; calf manna, so aromatic it must be good to eat; a rose garden, a honeysuckle vine and dozens of other blooms forming a potpourri of nature's fragrances; fresh baked bread, and the pungent aroma of a backyard barbecue. These are the things that intrude into brief moments of nostalgia just before you go to sleep; hopefully to dream.

Most of all you will rejoice at reuniting with your loved ones. They are still the same, but you must be careful not to bring the war home with you. They, like you, want to resume life as it was, and put the past behind the cover of the family album.

It's best if the returning prodigal can appear to be the same all-American kid that they knew so well. You are not, of course. But unless you're missing a limb or a lung, the return to the familiar homestead can be fairly quickly accomplished. The family can go on as it was in the past. The question is, can you?

* * * * *

I'm agoin' back to where I come from,
Where the honeysuckle smells so sweet it darn near makes you sick,
I used to think my life was humdrum,
But I sure as Hell can tell you that I learned real quick.

We used to go down to the station.

Just to watch the evenin' train come rollin' in,

And then one night, a great sensation,

Got the best of me and led me to a life of sin. Etc, etc.

This was one of maybe a hundred songs that Dick Whittington knew and would sing at the drop of an ice cube. I first knew Whittington when we were both going through the Air Corps' Advance Flying School at Aloe Field, Victoria, Texas. Finally, we both won our wings and he went to combat in twin engine A-20 attack bombers and I to England and P-51 fighters. Two years or so later we reunited aboard that old Liberty ship where we had finally gained a bed in a four-tiered bunk for our passage home from Le Havre to New York City.

After a brief layover at Camp Kilmer in New Jersey, we caught a C-54 flight west to Hayward Field across the bay from San Francisco where Dick was born and raised. We both kissed the tarmac at Hayward upon arrival, and spent the next couple of days at Camp Beale getting processed and honorably discharged. Still in uniform but now legal civilians, we had to celebrate.

And celebrate we did. Dick picked me up at the bus terminal in Oakland driving his dad's Packard sedan containing two quarts of Johnny Walker Black Label and two delightful young ladies, seniors at Mills College in Oakland. He introduced them; one as his cousin (my date), the other, her roommate.

We had a great evening; dinner at Fisherman's Wharf and the balance of the night at a beautiful Polynesian restaurant and lounge on the waterfront at Oakland where Dick and I horrified the waiter by drinking rare Scotch, and the ladies a variety of concoctions containing tiny Japanese umbrellas, miniature orchids and cunningly arranged fruit slices, and no booze.

It was the last party I was to attend in uniform and undoubtedly the best. We delivered our delightful companions to their quarters at Mills as the sun was coming up, and the plush Packard sedan made it slowly and safely to the Southern Pacific depot where I was due to depart in a couple of hours for Oregon.

"Mount Laki? You mean they say 'Mount Lake eye'?"

We shook hands and made promises to get together soon (which we never kept), and Whittington headed home.

"I was agoin' back to whar I come from."

* * * * *

My brother Paul met me at the railway station in Portland, and we didn't stop talking during the 26-mile drive to Newberg. Paul was the brother who was forced to stay at home during the war because he had been disabled with arthritis while still in his early twenties and was 4-F. His letters to me had indicated his strong vicarious feelings about my flying career in the air corps. His support was that of a loyal fan, and was a genuine inspiration to me.

Newberg hadn't changed. Main Street was still the site of almost all of the town's retail businesses. I was surprised when he pulled to the curb several blocks from Wiard Street, the north-south street that led to our home place a mile and a-half away. An appliance store fronted a two-story brick structure and to the right of the property was a handsome stairway entrance to an apartment above.

"The folks live here now, Alan," Paul said. "The ranch and the creamery were too much for Dad, and there was no manpower available for hire. This is a damn nice place and Mom and all of us are hoping Dad will get used to it."

Late that night after a great reunion celebration with my folks and all our local relatives and friends, I took a walk down the darkened, quiet Main Street and somehow wandered a few blocks north of town to the football field adjoining the campus of Pacific College. *I was thankful it hadn't changed.*

The ranch was gone, and with it a way of life that had been so dear to me. The animals . . . of course I knew Dad had found good homes for my two Alsatians, Kim-I and Pup (Kim-II). Babe, the Percheron mare that I'd fancied as my war horse, had found a stable with Walter Leth, the county agent and a close friend. The rest . . . the jersey milk herd, and the abundant wildlife still resided there.

I never went near the home place. I reluctantly realized that I possibly would not have been satisfied with the old life as a rancher, and I revived another dream that had long lurked in my mind. Broadcasting, journalism. Los Angeles was the place. *Thomas Wolfe was right.*

* * * * *

I abandoned any juvenile ideas I'd had about becoming a movie actor. Now, I had to make a living as a civilian. And no combat flight pay. I enrolled in a radio broadcasting school on Wilshire Boulevard and seemed to have a talent for newscasting. In a couple of months I was teaching the course, subbing for Bud Waite, a genuine NBC newsman. It was here that I met Carl Phillips, son of John Phillips, republican, and congressman for the California 21st District. They were building a new radio station, KPAS, at Banning, California, and I was hired as their commercial sales manager.

Although I did do considerable on-air newscasting, my primary duty was the sales-business end. I did this chore pretty well, but I wanted more action. I submitted resumes and audition records to stations in Oregon, and finally landed a job in Klamath Falls as news editor. Look out, Morrow, Sevareid and Cronkite . . . here I come.

"KFJI news interrupts this broadcast with a late breaking news bulletin hot off the wires of Associated Press. Dateline Tokyo, Japan, October 1, 1950. General Douglas MacArthur announced today that American Forces under his command launched a successful landing on the west coast of Korea at Inchon. Troops subsequently made a victorious march to the 38th Parallel and have complete control now of the entire Korean area south of that line. A detailed report will be aired on KFJI's Mutual Don Lee Network's World News at 6:00 P.M. We now resume the scheduled program in progress."

I waved to Ed Boyd, the board engineer in the control room just a few feet away from the glassed-in announce booth where I sat, and gave him a circled thumb and forefinger as he plugged in the network feed. I sat for a few minutes contemplating the report I had just announced. It was the best news release we'd had from the battle front since June 27 when President Truman had announced the "Police Action" we were taking in that far-off area. "Police Action, hell!

It's another damn war, and I'll bet some of my old buddies in the 357th Fighter Group are flying Mustangs over there right now."

Yet, at the same time I didn't have any strong feelings of guilt about not being in it. I felt like I'd paid my dues in England and Europe in WWII, and flying combat now in a fighter airplane out-dated by the new jets didn't hold much fascination. I'd heard P-51 Mustangs were flying ground support, strafing and dive bombing in Korea, and that the Mustang's liquid cooled in-line engine was not designed for that duty. Not only that, I'd finally made the transition back to civilian life after a couple of floundering years. I was having the time of my life, and no one was shooting at me.

Chapter IV

Call to Arms

Three WWII Air Force Reserve captains and an active duty major were once again contemplating combat duty in a new war in Korea. Captain Max Wauchope, Major George Kinney, and Captains Oliver Kinney and Alan Abner, all air force pilots, would soon be engaged in serving their country in a far-off continent.

The Kinney brothers, raised on ranches in Klamath County, Oregon, joined the Oregon National Guard in the late thirties to "train the draftees when the national conscription begins," as the army recruiter put it. They were called to active duty when WWII broke out and served in the ground forces where they both gained commissions. They later transferred to the air corps and won their wings. (They both served to retirement age as full colonels.)

Max Wauchope won his wings early in that war as an aviation cadet, was commissioned and flew long over-water missions in the Pacific Theater piloting a B-29 bomber. Subsequent to his discharge in 1946 he was recalled to active duty in 1950 to fly C-54 transport cargo planes again across the Pacific Ocean to Japan and Korea.

(He became a noted Oregon journalist and retired as city editor of *Portland Oregonian*.)

Like the Kinneys, I too joined the Oregon National Guard's 318th Field Artillery while still in high school. Luckily, I was not called to active duty when Pearl Harbor occurred, and I was able to enlist in the Army Air Corps where I won my wings and commission and finally flew combat with the 357th Fighter Group in the 8th Air Force in England.

From left to right, Capt. Max Wauchope, Maj. George Kinney,
Capt. Oliver Kinney, and Capt. Alan Abner

After this reunion, Major George Kinney rejoined his current outfit to continue what became a brilliant military career. We three "civilian captains" were soon to be recalled to active duty. All three of us were assigned to the Military Air Transport Service (MATS). After all, we'd had almost a four-year furlough to rest up.

Max Wauchope and I both returned to civilian careers at the end of the Korean War. Oliver Kinney, after devoting some seven years to military service, chose to pursue a career in the air force. In addition to his flying duties in WWII and Korea, he became a staff director of Airforce Transport Operation in the Pacific Theater during the Viet Nam War.

Perhaps the varied origins and careers of these four individuals from small towns and ranch backgrounds offer some endorsement for America's tradition of reliance on its citizen-soldiers in times of national crisis.

My changing ambitions while I was growing up ran from being a top rodeo contender, a boxing champion of the world in some as yet unknown weight category, an All American football player, or a movie actor. It wasn't until I was ready for college that I had decided on journalism as my life's work. I selected my academic majors with that in mind; English literature, history, psychology, and social sciences. A few years later my decision to get into radio broadcasting in 1946 after my discharge from active duty in WWII was a compromise. I could pursue a career in radio news reporting and at the same time get paid. It was all working out fairly well.

My private life was also proceeding nicely. I was able for the first time to expand my civilian wardrobe in a manner that allowed me to appear in public in a style expected of a small town "radio personality." I had shaved a half dozen strokes off my golf handicap by playing at least a couple of days a week. My old '36 Ford three-window coupe had been replaced by a year-old Ford convertible. Life in Klamath Falls, Oregon's fast lane was pretty slow but very enjoyable. And best of all, I had met a great lady who had agreed to marry me, the wedding date set for the first Sunday in November. All of these pleasant distractions caused me to be a little negligent in checking my personal mail regularly which resulted in slight com-plications of most of my personal plans.

On October 18, 1950, I opened an official envelope with an Oc-tober 10 postmark that contained a startling directive. It was from the United States Air Force and it ordered me to report to a USAF detachment in Portland, Oregon, on October 24, 1950, for processing and assignment to active duty.

Although some of my friends had volunteered for recall to ac-tive duty, I had not done so. I had long since ceased to be involved in a local Air Force Reserve Unit I had joined briefly. But this order demanded immediate obedience, and I responded accordingly. Dur-ing the next four days Donna and I were married, I unpacked my WWII officer's uniforms, gassed up the convertible, and we left in a cloud of Oregon summer dust for Portland.

The processing officer in Portland cleared me in short order, gave me the opportunity to enter active duty as a "Volunteer," which I accepted, and referred me to a flight surgeon who declared me fit for flying duty and other military assignments.

My new orders directed me to report forthwith to the Military Air Transport Service (MATS) at McChord Air Force Base, Tacoma, Washington.

MATS! Holy, Toledo, don't they know I am a fighter pilot? MATS is multi-engine transports, C-54s, C-119s, C-124s, C-47s. They've got to be kidding!

But they weren't.

* * * * *

"I will walk my post in a military manner." I will disregard the fact that it's rained for 30 days and 30 nights. And before that, it has rained for the preceding six months. I am protected from this infer-nal deluge by a parka that covers me from the top of my head to my knees. Below, my feet are soaked. I've got to get some boots or some kind of shoes that can wade around in puddles three inches deep for eight hours. What a way to fight a war; and from where I stood, there was no doubt there was a war going on.

I had been recalled in October, just three months after North Korea crossed the 38th Parallel, attacked South Korea, and President Truman declared a "Police Action," and American involvement in the conflict. I thought when I first received my orders to report for active duty that I would be joining a fighter group in the combat zone. To my surprise, I was instead assigned to this Military Air Transport unit. There were no fighter planes in MATS.

Ramp control officer was my primary designated duty. This job, though certainly an essential one, was a far cry from strapping on a P-51 Mustang and taking on the enemy in the skies over Europe as I had done just four short years ago. Of course this job was a helluva lot safer, but dull! I was suddenly ordered to be a *ground-pounder.*

I knew I was in for it the morning I reported for work to a Major Evans, my immediate commanding officer. I dressed carefully for the occasion, thinking I was reporting for duty at the operational, rather than a formal staff level. I was still in possession of my WWII dress uniform: forest green blouse, pink pants, brown boots, green shirt, tan tie, and of course a billed cap with a 50 mission crush. For this first "working assignment," however, I wore my treasured A-2 leather flight jacket with the 363rd Fighter Squadron insignia bravely displayed on the chest, and the 357th Fighter Group logo on the back. I thought the master sergeant who greeted me and smiled when I came in was properly impressed.

"Captain Abner, Alan K, A02059705, reporting for duty, Sir," I stated to a major sitting behind a desk, clicking my Wellington boot heels, saluting smartly, and standing at cadet-attention.

There was a long silence as Major Evans stared at me with a kind of glazed expression.

"Ah yes," he murmured. "Captain Abner." He said this with no words of welcome or any kind of greeting. Rustling a few papers on his desk, he finally found one that apparently applied to me and studied it.

"You will report to Captain Collins in Operations for briefing and your duty schedule." He paused and looked up at me with what I could only define as an expression of distaste.

"You have 30 days to equip yourself with the new regulation air force blue uniforms. I'd suggest you do so at the earliest opportunity. Dismissed."

I was still standing at attention, and though I was rather startled, I managed a correct salute, did a neat about face and beat a snappy retreat.

The sergeant smiled at me when I paused to ask him where Operations was located.

"It's two buildings down toward the ramp, Sir," he said. "The base quartermasters are on the other side of the field if you want to check out some 'reg' duds to work in. There's a half dozen uniform tailor shops in Tacoma for quality dress blues that I'll bet you are going to want. I personally prefer what you've got on."

I glanced at the sleeve of this friendly Mick and noticed a ladder of hash marks that indicated a lot of years of active duty.

"Thanks, Sarge," I said. "I guess it's that or a tour with Greyhound or the post office. The leather jacket was too much, huh?"

"Not for me, Cap'," he said. "It reminds me of the CBI and flyin' the Hump."

I was right. This old boy had seen some tough flying duty in the China-Burma Theater, and the "Hump" was the Himalayas, one of the toughest flying assignments in WWII. Now he was flying a desk!

* * * * *

The Ramp was about five acres of concrete located on the northwest corner of McChord AFB, Tacoma, Washington. It was here that dozens of C-54 transports planes, two or three at a time, arrived and departed 24 hours a day, providing the evacuation of casualties from the Korean War zone across the Pacific Ocean, and carrying cargo and personnel on their return to Tachikawa, Japan.

The weather at McChord during those winter months of 1950–1951 was generally foul, but the field was rarely closed down. The guys flying those giant transports were damn good instrument pilots, and an efficient Ground Control Assist (GCA) landing capability provided by the McChord radar specialists made all-weather operations routine.

I never ceased to be amazed at the consistent performance of the MATS system that would with regularity deliver an air evacuation flight within minutes of their estimated time of arrival after traversing a flight from halfway around the globe. Those trips departing from Tachikawa AFB, located a few miles from Tokyo, took the northern route and would fly for eight hours well off the coast of the eastern shores of the Soviet Union, past the Sea of Okhotsk to the American Aleutian Island chain that marks the division of the Bering Sea from the North Pacific. This first landing is at Shemya, a small island at the very end of the Aleutians where fog with winds up to 40 mph was not unusual. This was the end of the long, over-water final leg on the journey to their next destination, another eight-hour flight to Elmendorf AFB at Fairbanks, Alaska. Finally, the last 1,200-mile leg, on a southeasterly route to our base at Tacoma.

These maximum effort flights, almost always in bad weather conditions, and always over water, were nearly incomprehensible to me. I'd flown missions out of England in lousy weather, but we usually broke out on top of the overcasts in less than an hour, and the time crossing the English Channel was measured in minutes.

Can you imagine the dogged endurance and the tenacious devotion to duty the crews of these C-54 transport crews exhibited day after day? And consider the ordeal of the patients and the nurses attending them that endured the entire flight without relief.

I knew there was a real war going on all right. The evidence was dramatically presented to me each night of duty as a ramp control officer.

* * * * *

I don't like to think it was because I was a kind of lame duck fighter pilot that I soon was locked in on supervising the ramp control swing shift from 4:00 P.M. to midnight. I didn't mind the hours as I'd been a night person before my recall to active duty, working as I had as a full-time civilian radio broadcaster. And I can truthfully say I didn't mind not flying at night and in weather that was not habit-forming.

My duties soon became routine, but each night offered some diversion.

The arrival of each flight followed a prescribed pattern. A time was entered on my log noting the hour and the minute the chocks, triangular pieces of wood, were braced against the tires of the aircraft. The plane would be scheduled for departure in two hours.

During this brief period, the litters carrying the patients would be off-loaded and carefully transferred to the waiting ambulances that would transport them to Madigan Hospital located on the Fort Lewis Military Reservation just a half hour away. As soon as this was completed, cargo would be removed by a civilian cargo crew, and when off-loading was completed, they would immediately load the cargo standing by all ready on floats for the scheduled "turn around" next trip assignment to Japan.

Upon arrival, a maintenance ground crew man would consult with the pilot and the crew chief for repairs or adjustments that might be needed. The fuel trucks were in place almost when the props stopped turning refilling the C-54 tanks with one-hundred octane gas.

When the loading of cargo was completed and the cargo chief had determined that the weight and balance of the load was accurately located to assume the proper flying altitude of the aircraft, and all other services had been completed, I would make the inspections and then sign off the completion documents and await the arrival of the crew.

Finally, with the crew aboard, and when any service personnel passengers who were "sandbagging" back to the war zone were strapped in, the engines were started, the chocks removed, and all systems were go.

My last official function was to stand at attention about 50 feet, diagonally from the front and to the pilot's side of the aircraft and salute that face above me in the pilot's window. He was clear to taxi.

That was the end of my responsibilities to this link in the air-evac chain, and the beginning of another long flight for that pilot and his crew.

My last entry in the log for each "turnaround" was the chock time at release. MATS was quite serious about the requirement that the elapsed time on my ramp for any Air-evac C-54s did not exceed two hours. We rarely violated this curfew.

I must admit that though I was respectful of the seriousness of my ramp control assignment, I felt I was more of a spectator rather than a participant in a very important process. At times I felt as I had on numerous previous occasions when I had been a news reporter covering a big story. Having been a combat fighter pilot, I suppose I was frustrated at not being able to come to closer grips with the enemy that caused the distress I witnessed each night when those wounded combat casualties were brought in. This continual exposure to the pain of war was a real stimulant to my increasing frustration and anger at not being more actively involved.

Chapter V

Flying Time

The swing shift did offer some off-duty time for daylight diversion. Although I was on flying status there was certainly little opportunity to solo in the single engine category for which I was authorized. There were no F-51 Mustangs on the base or even an AT-6 trainer that I could check out for a local flight. Like other pilots I had known, I found that nothing smoothed out the tensions of mundane ground duties like getting aloft in a fighter or trainer aircraft and "wringing it out." To escape the confines of earth-bound routines and swoop and roll in the limitless skies was true relief.

The day I arrived at McChord AFB I had witnessed a scramble of a number of fighters based there by a group attached to the Air Defense Command. From across the field where I first saw them I thought from the side view silhouette that they were Mustangs. The needle nose, the square tail, and the sound of that beautiful in-line engine. "Ah hah!" I thought. "At last."

My delight was soon shattered. When the fighters turned in the air after take-off I saw what at first looked like a flight of four F-51s in the tightest formation I'd ever witnessed. It wasn't four single-engine Mustangs, it was two twin-engine aircraft, types that I did not know existed. They were F-61s, a hybrid kind that some ingenious designer had conceived by joining two Mustangs into one P-38-like fighter. The right wing of one was shortened and joined to a similarly cropped left wing of another. A broad horizontal tail assembly had likewise been adapted and attached to the tail ends of the twin fuselages, and two square vertical rudders completed the profile. They sort of resembled the P-38 Starfire. The air arm of the United States was changed in 1947 from the U.S. Army Air Corps to the United States Air Force. Many changes were made, including new blue uniforms, and pursuit (P) planes were designated fighter (F) craft.

"What in hell have they done? What is this monstrosity? Why would they ruin the best fighter plane in the world?"

I soon learned some of the answers to my initial complaints. The F-61 was now said to be the fastest prop-driven airplane in existence. It doubled the efficiency of its operational capabilities by having a crew of two persons rather than a single all-purpose pilot. It was truly a formidable aerial weapon.

But it was a twin-engine aircraft, and I was not qualified to fly in it as I was single-engine rated. I decided to get twin-engine qualified, so I gained the acquaintance of a Lieutenant Breitenstein who was our outfit's C-47 expert. Breit' was a real barnstormer type who could fly the "Gooneybird" like no one I'd ever met. On our final flight he demonstrated what his old kite could do, and it was not unlike the first rides I'd taken in flying school trainers. He executed power on and power off stalls, wheels down stalls, lazy eights, and finally to my amazement, a barrel roll. I was impressed. I also decided to wait a while to make my transition to twin-engine aircraft.

* * * * *

During that winter of 1950–51 I did manage to get in enough monthly flying time to qualify for flight pay: a couple of hops to the MATS bases in Great Falls, Montana; a trip to Wright Patterson, Ohio; a couple to Travis AFB near Sacramento, California; and a trip to Edwards AFB north of Los Angeles—all in the right seat of a C-47 as a copilot. Swell!

Someone in Operations decided I should fly a route indoctrination run to Elemendorf AFB in Alaska with the view that I could then clear flight plans for Air Evacuation MATS flights to that destination. I had an Operations MOS from my former WWII duties with the 357 Fighter Group, and I was hopeful I might make the transition to an assignment in Operations from Ramp Control.

I responded to the flight line at 2300, met the crew in Operations preparing their flight plan, and boarded the loaded C-54 with them in time for a 2400 take-off for Elemendorf AFB, Anchorage, Alaska. As third pilot I sand-bagged the take-off and climb-out seated with the flight engineer in the pilot's compartment. When we reached our assigned altitude and had taken up our northerly heading, the command pilot put the craft on auto pilot, told the copilot to vacate the right seat and waved for me to take it.

"Watch the store for a bit, Cap'," he said to me. "I'm going to grab a little nap. Holler if you need help."

I slid into the right side copilot's seat, put on the radio headset, and fastened my seat belt.

I really thought at first that this was some sort of practical joke. Ah ha, I thought. This truck driver is going to spook a smart-ass fighter jock, hey? Well, he can suck air before I wake him up yelling uncle! So I immediately began to check the instrument readings. Air speed 180 indicated, 2,000 RPMs, altitude 9,000 feet, heading 320 degrees, 30 inches manifold pressure. The props were in sync, so I had no problem with them. The auto pilot was on, and I'd watched him tweak the altitude and directional knobs, so I figured I could maintain course and altitude.

The sky was clear and no danger or indication of any icing problems. And when I radioed our position at the first route checkpoint, giving our position, our home station, our destination, present time, and the ETA to Elemendorf AFB I felt that things were under control and began to relax.

The only thing that bothered me was our heading, 320 degrees. As a kid I knew where the big dipper and the north star were. That was North, and that's where Santa came from, and that was where Alaska was! My brain and the instruments told me that we were correct in our heading, but my instincts nagged at me that we were flying out over the North Pacific Ocean.

I subdued my childhood recollections and was starting to really begin to relax and enjoy the beautiful starlit night and the smooth ride. It was then I noticed the early signs of daybreak appearing at about four o'clock, to the right of our nose. The sun rises in the East, Godammit! What in hell is it doing coming up there? For just a moment, I was completely rattled.

This sunrise was really spectacular. It was when a jagged shaft of brilliant light stabbed up into the heavens that I realized what I was seeing. Like the religious revival convert who exclaimed, "I saw the light"; the old man who cries, "Like a bolt out of the blue." It came to me. "Then came the dawn," as an answer appears to a complex problem. It's the northern lights, dummy!

I had never seen the aurora borealis, and nothing I'd ever heard about it had prepared me for the magnificence of the display. It was truly mind-boggling. I knew this visual and emotional experience, even with its humorous overtones, would be a tale I'd be likely to tell for years to come.

I would not, however, relate it to the command pilot a few inches away when he finally would awaken from his nap, or the crew members, or anyone else in MATS.

Chapter VI

Class Action

"What in hell is psychological warfare?" The question I posed to Donna was not rhetorical. The reason I asked was because of a piece of paper I held that had been handed me when I got off duty at midnight. The document was a new set of orders directing me to report for temporary duty (TDY) to Headquarters Air Resupply and Communications Service (ARCS), Washington, D.C., to attend Georgetown University in that city for training in a psychological warfare course of instruction. As usual, it was short notice. I had five days to report for duty.

The next morning I requested and was granted permission to meet with Colonel Richard Bromley, our wing commander, whom I had assisted on a number of occasions in preparing him for appearances on KING-TV in Seattle on a weekly air force public relations appearance. I had a lot of respect for the colonel, a really great guy, and I hoped he would enlighten me on this new assignment.

"It's a new program the air force is embarking on, Alan," he said. "As you may know, the army has been involved in tactical psywar for some time out of Fort Benning, Georgia. Apparently our interest is in developing a capability for the air force in strategic psywar materials and techniques in warfare psychologically waged. I endorsed your selection for the Georgetown program some time ago when your name was submitted to me. I gathered this career change was contemplated when you were recalled to active duty because of your civilian career as a broadcaster and newsman. I've wondered why an old fighter jock like you was assigned to us. Now, I guess, we know."

At last a mystery was solved that had baffled me for some time. Last summer, before I had been recalled, I had gotten several queries from old friends and classmates I hadn't heard from in years calling or writing me asking some curious questions. "Hey Ab. Have you robbed a bank or what?" "A guy, I think he was FBI, was here asking about you the other day. Said it was just a routine check." "Captain Abner, a government agent inquired about your scholastic records which we gave him."

Colonel Bromley said this was usual procedure for the military to use the services of the bureau (FBI) to do background checks on personnel to be qualified for TOP SECRET security clearances.

"I have no doubt," the colonel said, "that the Psychological Warfare program will require people in it to have TOP SECRET clearances."

Ah hah! That explains it. That's why I was assigned to MATS rather than to duty as a fighter pilot. I was relieved to learn all of this, and I'm sure Major Evans, my short term CO, would have been equally re-assured that he wasn't going to be required to staff his Ramp Control with hot-shot ex-fighter jocks.

I thanked the colonel for the bombshell he had dropped on me. So now they tell me! After months pounding the rain-soaked pavement on the ramp at McChord, I learned what in hell I was doing in MATS. I also found out that I would be assigned to the ARCS, a division of MATS, on temporary duty (TDY), and my primary duty would be to graduate level classes at Georgetown University, a name that brought chills down my spine. Hot damn! Talk about luck. I couldn't have imagined a better military assignment than this one.

When Donna and I were married we had scrapped all of our plans for a big bash wedding, and had settled for a small private ceremony conducted by Reverend Tweet of the Klamath Falls Lutheran Church. Again, we were pressed for time. Five days to report for duty across the entire United States. Of course, the air force expected me to fly. But I wanted my bride with me; the Ford was nearly new, so Tally Ho the fox, let's get packed, and get going.

We stored our few furnishings and extra wardrobe in a Tacoma warehouse owned by my brother Don, had Emma, Donna's mother, pick up Terry, our poodle, and we peeled off before dawn with three days left to traverse nearly three thousand miles by car.

Our first stop en route from Tacoma was a small motel a few miles north of Chicago. We had shared driving but were getting tired enough to be dangerous, so we crashed for an eight-hour rest stop.

I was taking a nap late in the afternoon of the third day while Donna flew the Ford, and was pleased as I awakened when Donna announced we were on the outskirts of Washington, some seven or eight hours early. We relaxed for the first time since our departure when we realized we had a night to recover before reporting in the next morning. We stopped on the outskirts of the city, had a leisurely lunch and then looked for a place to rest. We were still in what I viewed as a suburban part of the District, when I saw a Chamber of Commerce building. Inquiring of the nice lady on duty as to the location of Georgetown University, we were surprised when she opened a huge atlas and drew a line with her finger that went across both pages.

"Let's see," she said. "Georgetown's in the District of Columbia and is located here in the southwest part of that city."

We were in Washington, Pennsylvania!

We made it to the door before we collapsed in a gale of laughter bordering on hysteria. We made it to the car with me limping from a dollar size blister on my right foot, and Donna hanging on to me with eyes and nose dripping from a rather severe sinus ailment.

"Hey. We've got it made. Only four more hours to go," I said when we had somewhat recovered.

It was more like seven hours, when we finally called it quits and found a hostel on Wisconsin Avenue in the capital city and checked in about midnight.

After a shower, we decided we should find the ARCS headquarters at 2400 Newark Street then so I wouldn't have any difficulty locating it at 8:00 in the morning.

I followed the directions given us by the landlady of the Bide a Wee lodge, and we found Newark Street with little difficulty.

We slowly traversed north on Newark Street, reading addresses in the dim early morning light. Finally, there it was.

Rising three steps from the curb was a pile of concrete steps with the numbers 2400 blazoned on the front. That was it. The rest of the location was a vacant lot.

We sat there, stunned, for a couple of minutes. Our entire trek across the United States had turned into a sort of hazy nightmare. Now this.

"I sort of figured," I said, "that this psychological warfare business would be classified Top Secret. But this is carrying secrecy a bit far. This comes close to that old security gag about 'burn before reading.'"

We finally learned from an all-night service station attendant that Newark was divided in two parts by Rock Creek Park, and we were in the wrong section. We finally found the ARCS's Headquarters building about 3:00 A.M., and five hours later I reported there on time, only to be told that I wouldn't be needed for a week or so, and to check in daily by phone. Now they tell me!

Washington, D.C., in 1951 was a delightful town. The war caused the usual housing shortages in the nation's capital as it does in times of conflict. But we finally found furnished quarters in an old apartment complex called Cathedral Mansions. A mansion it wasn't, but it was well situated fairly close to ARCS Headquarters and also to Georgetown University. But the best feature was its location just across the street from the Smithsonian Institute park and zoo where we spent what little free daytime leisure we were to have during our stay.

We soon learned that one of the neighbors on our floor was Lieutenant Bill Burkhart and his charming wife, Manuela. Burkhart was also in the psywar program with me, and we greatly enjoyed their company. Manuela was of Rumanian descent and had some difficulty with some of the pronunciation of complicated English words. Visits to the nearby zoo resulted in her reports of seeing some very strange animals: "hitsapotamoas," "jeer-afefs" and the classic "rhinosaucer-wasis." I couldn't help but be impressed by the difficulties we undoubtedly would presently face in psywar with materials designed to persuade peoples of various nationalities to react to a variety of psywar stimuli. I was confident Georgetown's famous school of languages and linguistics would provide the answers to this problem.

* * * * *

I must admit I was somewhat intimidated by the quality of the other student officers listed on the roster I saw who were scheduled for the Georgetown graduate course the air force had arranged for psywar trainees. The list included a large segment of new second lieutenant ROTC graduates the Air Force had gleaned from the previous year's outstanding students graduating from universities all over the United States. They held B.A. and B.S. degrees in such fields as psychology, social sciences, economics, history, foreign affairs, social psychology, languages, and various nationality areas, and others in the humanities categories.

The next segment was made up of a couple of dozen M.A.s and a smaller group of Ph.D.s in similar fields.

Finally, a group of individuals from the military that included majors, lieutenant colonels, and colonels whose credentials qualified them for this career change.

As a captain with no apparent military career ambitions, I hardly fit into this last category. And as an academic my college career had been interrupted a couple of times by WWII, and though I had enough scattered credits for a degree, I had never graduated from a university, and did not own a single college level sheepskin. Luckily, my credits and my civilian occupation seemed to have had some influence on my selection, and Georgetown granted me an academic equivalence B.A. status to qualify me for their graduate school program. It appeared I had progressed from the lame duck fighter pilot of the Military Air Transport Service to the ugly duckling of ARCS.

* * * * *

The scene was a marvelous restaurant setting the officials at ARCS Headquarters had arranged to greet and entertain the hundred or so officers that had been selected for the Georgetown psywar training program. Except for a few representatives from the university, we were all in uniform and I'd never seen so many high-ranking officers up close in my military career. Each speaker that greeted us had done so in a warm, casual way that created an almost clublike atmosphere that relaxed all of us. The luncheon had reached the dessert stage, most of the bemedaled dignitaries had spoken briefly, and the colonel who was acting as the master of ceremonies made a final invitation.

"Gentlemen," he said. "We are aware of the interesting, indeed impressive backgrounds many of you bring to this gathering. I'm sure it would be enlightening to all of us to hear any remarks any of you would care to make before we adjourn. Knowing your successful academic and military backgrounds, and that you have already demonstrated a competitive attitude, we would like to bestow on the person making the most impressive short speech, an appropriate trophy. We don't expect a scholastic dissertation, but perhaps a description of your home town, an interesting experience, even a joke would be acceptable." The colonel held up a stuffed creature that we all recognized as a Schmoo, the cartoon creation by Al Capp featured in his popular comic strip, Lil Abner. This two-foot Schmoo was in the Georgetown colors of blue and gray and displayed the university's logo on his ample belly.

A number of guests responded to the invitation to speak and made brief remarks, mostly from the ranks of the new junior lieutenants, and many of them were quite humorous but still respectful.

The colonel MC then made a comment that for a moment chilled my blood.

"I've noticed that among us is a namesake of the comic strip owner of the object of this competition, the famous Schmoo. Captain Alan Abner is that person, and I'm sure we'd enjoy his comments."

Why I chose in that moment of near panic the subject I selected, I'll never know.

"I'd first like to welcome you new officers in the United States Air Force," I began. "I know you must be awed as I am with the impressive display of rank and ribbons that are represented here today. I know many of you are already thinking about promotion to a higher grade, but I recently had a brief encounter that might illustrate the difficulties that could befall you along the way.

"I was at the bar at the Andrews Air Force Base Officers' Club the other evening, having my customary Dr. Pepper, when I met a first lieutenant pilot I'd not seen since flying school many years ago. I couldn't help but wonder why this rather morose old friend was still a first lieutenant. He downed his, I believe, second drink and told me.

"'I was stationed in Australia,' he said, 'well out of a combat zone, flying with a Fighter Group that had a commander that loved to call a practice alert at all hours of the night, every night. It was driving us all nuts. Well, I got a pass to Sydney, and while there I acquired an orangutan from a street show that was going out of business. I brought him back to the base under wraps, and in no time I had him trained. He was very smart. When the alert would sound in the middle of the night, he'd jump out of his bed, put on my flight jacket, helmet and goggles, and race down to the flight line and sit in my airplane until the all clear sounded.

"'Boy, it went real well, until one night I heard our planes taking off. It was an actual alert! I ran outside just in time to see my plane taking off with the orangutan flying it.' My friend took a long sip of his drink. 'Well, you can guess the rest,' the first lieutenant said. 'That's the reason I'm still a first lieutenant. There's one thing that rankles me though. That damn orangutan is now a lieutenant colonel in the Pentagon.'"

Well, I must modestly say, that yarn brought down the house. I was relieved to note, that to a man, the lieutenant colonels and colonels were the loudest and most raucous of them all. The applause was deafening, and the Schmoo was mine. I thought that *Daisy Mae* might be quietly proud.

Chapter VII

Georgetown University

The first morning that classes were to begin, I got an early start and parked my tired Ford convertible just a block or so off campus. I was so impressed with the fact that I was attending this great university that I wanted to first get a feel of the campus. Walking decisively up and down the shaded streets I felt like I was literally moving through history. The stately ivy-covered buildings, built mostly of brick or stone, seemed to emanate an aura of scholarship and learning. I was somewhat awed by the prospect of belonging, if only for a brief time, to the historic roster of those students that had been privileged to study and just to be here.

When my first class convened, I was at once delighted with the collegiate atmosphere of the large lecture hall. All of us were in civilian clothes, rank was not discernible, and the result was the creation of a large, but typical congregation of graduate level participants.

The titles of the various areas included in the curriculum of the course were not particularly intimidating. We now learned, however, that the depth into which each subject was developed was far from superficial. Almost without exception, each category was probed by a noted expert in their fields that went far beyond the usual academic range.

The curriculum included political theory, propaganda, area study (general), area study (specific), social psychology, intelligence, public opinion, Russia, communism, and anticommunist techniques.

Great lecturers were often called to address many of these classes who had particular experience or expertise that enhanced the range and depth of the subject matter. Continual emphasis was made in each category on the practical application of the subject, and not just a pedantic dissertation in the abstract. We never lost sight of the anticipated application of this knowledge and that we would eventually be charged in creating additional military capability for the defeat of an enemy.

It now seems strange to me that until then I had no real understanding of what the term "psychological warfare" could encompass. I had a vague idea that it involved the dropping of leaflets on troops, and in some cases, civilian populations. I'd seen newsreels of helicopters in actual war zones equipped with public address systems haranguing enemy troops on the ground. I supposed these efforts were designed to effect the disaffection and hopefully, desertion of military individuals opposing us, and in some cases, causing confusion and even rebellion of soldiers toward their leaders.

I was aware to some extent of warfare psychologically waged. One only had to recall the London Blitz of WWII that I had witnessed personally to understand the Nazi strategy of submission. The Allies' own policy that later resulted in the widespread bombing of cities within the Third Reich's control was for similar reasons. Not only was the morale of the populace affected, but the broad disruption of the production of military machines and material was initially important to the deterrence of the enemy's ability to continue resistance to our more conventional military efforts.

These examples of psywar were apparent to me in having witnessed some of them previously, and other occasions that one could recall from other historic conflicts. But I was really not aware of the potential that was available to heighten sophisticated psywar efforts. I was soon to be exposed to at least an introduction to this manner of waging war.

I for one, and I suspect others recruited into this new program, had a rather uneasy feeling that "psychological warfare" had a rather sinister connotation. Propaganda was a word that was familiar in the context of the lies and distortions that were disseminated in WWI and more recently by Herr Goebbels and the Nazis. It was rather a relief to at least learn the origins of the term.

It was appropriate that our exposure to propaganda took place at Georgetown, one of America's foremost Catholic universities. The word had its origins in a historic section of the Catholic Church that was assigned the task for the disseminating of Catholicism in non-Catholic countries. It was called the Sacred Congregation for the Propagation of the Faith, instituted by A Papal Bull and was composed of thirteen cardinals and two prelates, a secretary, and a consultor; the date, 1650.

The Roman Church's early monopoly over the propagation of religious ideas was undermined to some extent in the 15th century with the invention of the printing press and the emergence of the Protestant Revolution. Additional factors were introduced during the Renaissance, also the era of exploration, that resulted in the finding of new continents and finally, the Industrial Revolution.

In America's colonial period, political propaganda gained new momentum in the years before the Revolutionary War. Samuel Adams utilized his Committees of Correspondence, as well as Tom Paine's effective writings. Even the new U.S. Constitution resulted in the new arguments presented by the Federalist Papers. I was somewhat intellectually stimulated by the attendance it offered to the grim solutions the world had long relied upon by using technologically effective machines and methods in the killing of each country's youth on both sides, and ultimately winning at such a great cost of human life. Was it possible that such contests could be won by persuasion rather than the traditional methods?

It developed that we were to consider ways to not only supplement the efforts already being made to win this war, but to possibly lay the groundwork for a new emphasis in conceiving operational overlay plans that gave more consideration to the psychological aspects of preventing wars, waging them if they became necessary, and then implementing these new elements in the occupation of conquered areas, and winning the subsequent peace.

Georgetown University was the ideal place for the consideration and development of this new concept of military operations. Within the university's sphere of learning were the schools of Foreign Service, Languages and Linguistics.

Our daytime schedule constituted what could accurately be described as a "Crash Course." The sessions began at 8:30 A.M. and continued to 5:30 P.M., Monday through Friday, with an hour for lunch. I soon learned that the lecture requirements also demanded at least four hours of additional study and research after school hours at night. Weekends were used in catching up with the loose ends that remained.

I loved every minute of it. Every hour spent in the classroom was pertinent and to the point. There was no long convoluted academic theorizing. Each speaker was an expert in his field, and applied his specific expertise to the practical general goals of the course.

The study of psychology had held an early interest for me in my previous collegiate career. I had spent a couple of years wrestling with it, and finally had more or less rejected it as an "inexact science." It seemed to me that the behavior of individuals was largely based on arguable theory and did not meet the usual provable standards required in other sciences.

I was relieved to now "discover" social psychology, the study of the behavior of individuals in groups. Here at last, was something I could believe in, and that I could readily grasp as a practical means of analyzing the elements of group dynamics, and anticipating ways that could be utilized in manipulating group reactions to stimuli.

The principle text used was one by Krech and Crutchfield, and the collaboration of these two experts in the field was enhanced by their drawing to a great extent on dozens of other scientists and practitioners. I was interested in a paragraph from the opening preface to the text.

"Basic principles and theory frequently prove bothersome to the teacher whose students are not going to become professional psychologists but who are primarily interested in practical applications.

A large section of this book is devoted to such practical applications, but if the student is to 'get' that material he must first take the necessary time to spend the mental energy to assimilate and understand the basic principles discussed."

This was an accurate description of the "student" in our case, and the reference to "time" and "energy" was a fair warning as to what the course would require.

I was well aware of the dangers of relying on a *little knowledge* of a technical matter. But I was determined that I would become knowledgeable enough to select and then rely on the advice and guidance of real experts to create practical operational plans and materials.

The course was a delight, and one had the feeling that the hours devoted to it were indeed time well spent.

Chapter VIII

Secret Witness

The deep tone of a chime somewhere in the campus sounded the half-hour, and as if that was a cue, the door in front and the left side of the large classroom opened and a tall figure entered. He mounted the steps up to the raised lecture platform and proceeded to the table in the center where he placed his hat, a gray homburg, and a briefcase. He still hadn't looked at the silent audience.

"Good morning, Gentlemen," he said, with a slight accent that was unidentifiable, except that it was probably European.

"I am Jan Karski, and I am here to inform you about the humanitarianism of German Nazis, and the benevolent nature of America's former allies, the Russian communists."

There was an almost audible gasp from the silent assembly, and then a crooked smile illuminated his gaunt face. The place erupted in an appreciative roar of laughter.

This was Jan Karski, who in those few introductory words set the tone for what proved to be the most informative and entertaining series of lectures I, and I suspect most of us, had ever witnessed.

The course titles he was assigned were twofold: Russia, and Communism, and Anti-Communist Techniques. The two courses were intertwined and were further augmented by a colorful review of the history of the powers that contributed to our current wartime situation.

Karski came to us with impressive credentials. He was a 25-year-old Polish cavalry officer in 1939 when Poland was attacked, first by Germany, and a few weeks later by Russia. A graduate of the

University of Lwow in 1935, he had been lecturing at the University of Warsaw in demographics, his academic specialty, when the Nazi *Luftwaffe* attacked, and troops and tanks crossed the German-Polish border on September 1. Less than three weeks later, the Ribbentrop-Molotov pact was announced, and Russian troops crossed into Poland, occupied portions of it, and Karski, along with hundreds of his comrades, was loaded into boxcars and shipped to labor camps in Russia. He escaped and began years of activity with the Polish underground, fighting both the Nazis and the Communists. The scars on his wrists bore testimony to the torture he suffered during this period when he was tortured by the Gestapo, and made an attempt to end his life rather than betray his country.

During the closing years of WWII he became a courier between the Polish underground and the Polish government in exile in London headed by Prime Minister General Igor Sigorski. During this period he met with Churchill, Anthony Eden, and nearly every other English political leader. In 1943 at Roosevelt's request he reported to the president on the horrors of the concentration camps he had personally observed in Germany and Russia. He was honored with Poland's highest military order, and decorated with the Cross of the Virtuti Militari.

His lectures not only described the intricacies of communist dialectic materialism, but suggested ways of counteracting their theories, and described techniques that could be useful in subverting their influence on the North Korean counterpart.

* * * * *

It was my first taste of vodka. I wondered if I could ever acquire a taste for it. I had successfully conditioned my palate to scotch whiskey during my tenure in England during WWII, but this stuff had little taste and plenty of heat. It was imported vodka, probably Polish, and I guessed about 100 proof. It was served neat in what at first looked like a jelly glass, but on closer inspection I could see was a 3- or 4-ounce crystal tumbler. I was a little confused because I didn't know whether to toss it off neat, or sip it. I watched our host and noticed his technique was something in between a gulp and a short drink. By the third drink I had mastered the proper method. But I'm not too certain about my performance after handling additional servings.

Our host was Jan Karski, and he was most hospitable. To save us from what I'm certain would have been a gustatory disaster, he supplied a generously loaded tray of a variety of cheeses and cold meats and slices of a dark, coarse rye bread that provided some balance to the liquid part of the menu.

Our last class each day was "Russia," and occasionally, usually on Friday, Jan would invite a few of his many student fans to stop by his apartment on Wisconsin Avenue after class for a "weekender," as we called it.

Karski was a marvelous raconteur, and we all considered it a privilege to associate with this remarkable man on a social level. Warsaw, pre-war, seemed to have been something like Paris. Karski's life was one of satisfying intellectual challenge, yet at the same time, filled with an exciting round of theatre, concerts, opera, restaurants and night clubs, and sufficient romantic activity to fully occupy a young bachelor in his mid-twenties.

It was clear that he enjoyed reminiscing about these early years, but always in the background was our knowledge of the terrible fate that had awaited him. There was about him a certain latent Slavic sadness that lingered just beneath a veneer of convivial behavior. There was nothing of the melancholy during these sessions. In fact it was a typical bull session filled with ribald narratives and much laughter. It was a happy combination of intelligent company enjoying a welcome break from more serious pursuits.

Professor Karski's Georgetown "tea times" usually lasted only a couple of hours, and on one occasion my merry comrades and I saying our *Bon Soirs*, reeling slightly out into a now dark rainy evening, piled into my recently acquired '49 Buick Roadmaster convertible. As the senior ranking officer and the owner of the car I, of course, drove. My crew, four second lieutenants, knew I was a pilot, and there was a good deal of interrogation about my ability to navigate after dark, and of course whether I was trained in foul-weather flying. But I manfully ignored their heckling, and splashed down the river that was named Wisconsin Avenue.

This thoroughfare had a cunning characteristic that I'd never seen before. At infrequent intervals there are islands, pointed on the end facing the traffic, shaped like an elongated narrow pie about three feet wide, eight or ten inches high, and twenty or so feet long. They are located in the street about ten feet from the curb. I supposed they were remnants of earlier days when street cars went down the middle of the street, but now they are there for passengers waiting to board a bus.

I was not aware that I had misjudged my entrance into the narrow lane on the right of the island, and was amazed when I hit an almost indiscernible tiny sign on a thin rod standing at the end of the island. I was straddling the island, but with the finely honed instincts of a seasoned fighter pilot, I stopped quickly.

My intrepid crew bailed out of the craft into the continuing downpour. I backed up, and except for the broken lens on the left front headlight, there was no other discernible damage. One of my more imaginative mates quickly retrieved the sign and placed it carefully in some shrubbery bordering the sidewalk.

As we quickly re-entered the vehicle, a police patrol car pulled in behind us. Two officers approached on foot, one of whom quickly discovered the broken headlight lens, the glass in the island, and the other officer clearly spotted the bent sign peering from the bushes.

There was no interrogation, just a terse "follow me," and we headed for the Georgetown police station.

It soon developed that I was not without legal counsel. Two of my associates were obviously well versed on illegal search and seizure, another on habeas corpus, and finally, a constitutional rights expert!

I managed to isolate my bibulous barristers in the ante room outside the station desk area where I, after a little small talk, discovered the sergeant in charge, a guy about my age, had been a crew chief on P-47 Thunderbolts in the 9th Air Force in WWII.

He finally made a very intelligent decision. "Get those bums out of here. Your car will be here in our parking lot. You can pick it up in the morning."

My final words to my partners in crime were: "I managed to get a stay on our case. But I promise you, I'll fight this thing right up to the juvenile court."

The final couple of weeks of our Georgetown assignment were devoted primarily to seminar sessions in each of the courses, where smaller groups of six or eight students were gathered with the instructor to review and discuss the subject matter involved. There were written final examinations in most classes. I supposed the air force probably required this action in order to determine how effective the instruction had been and how the various students ranked in their performance scholastically. I had experienced no difficulty in any of the tests and felt I had reached a new high in my college experience up until now. I must admit that for the first time I was extremely interested in all of the subject matter I was exposed to, and certainly motivated by the prospect of how we might put this new knowledge to work.

The university staged a marvelous reception for us at the end of the term. It was held in a huge room on campus, and for the final time since our arrival we gathered dressed in our class A uniforms. Rank had long since ceased to exist in the classroom, and I was startled to know that Carl, a fellow student some twenty years my senior, a person I assumed was an academic of some stripe, and who had been seated next to me in most of my classes, turned out to be a full colonel. We had our first informal conversation on this occasion, and I learned he too had started his career in the Army Air Corps as a fighter pilot. He'd flown the early P-36 pursuit plane in Hawaii, and General Laurence Norstadt, the air force chief of staff, had been his flying mate in a squadron stationed at Hickam Field in Honolulu. Carl, or rather Colonel Swyter, was a great guy, and Donna and I became good friends with him and his wife, Peggy, later during our tour of duty with ARCS.

The final festive occasion held by Jan Karski was a small party for about eight or ten of his students and their wives or lady friends. Donna was as impressed with the Polish hero as I was. He was a man of great grace and charm, and his continental style in entertaining his guests was a fitting climax to our delightful stay at Georgetown University.

Chapter IX

Propaganda

"There are probably hundreds of people who know more about psychological warfare than I do. But, I don't see any of them here, so I'll proceed as the instructor of this class in the techniques and materials that can be used in the area of radio broadcasting in the disseminating of psywar messages."

I was somewhat intimidated by my new assignment to teach this course to the thirty or so psywarriors who sat facing me. After completion of the Georgetown University indoctrination, 86 graduates had been ordered to Mountain Home Air Force Base, Idaho, for further practical training in this new military concept. The campus for this school was a former WWII air corps training facility located at Gowen Field, Boise, Idaho.

I managed to stay a chapter ahead of a lecture manual that was provided me, but I soon found that even though the class was rather large, a seminar environment was more productive in developing new approaches to the subject matter. These were very bright young men, and they readily became enthusiastic in applying their own area of expertise in economics, psychology, sociology, etc., to innovative new applications to the subject.

The scope of our discussions was not limited to just the usual utilization of radio broadcasting as we know the civilian medium. Some of the techniques common in the commercial broadcast style had been in use for a long time by Radio Free Europe and The Voice of America. The hallmark of these efforts' credibility was truth. Provable truth. The only news that vast audiences in Central and Eastern

Europe had access to was provided by these operations. We knew there were thousands of concealed AM and short wave radio receivers throughout the entire region. This was an existent avenue of access to these vulnerable listeners. The fact that these people owned a radio set indicated a certain amount of disaffection and distrust of state-owned media that could be exploited. It would seem to be a waste to permit the good will these two existing broadcasters had created over the years, but this was war, and every means available to win had to be considered.

There is little evidence to indicate that the WWII broadcasts of Germany's "Berlin Calling" by the English renegade Lord Haw Haw, or Japan's Tokyo Rose had any significant effect on the morale of Allied troops. But the fact that Goebbels and the Japanese propaganda experts considered it a worthwhile endeavor offered some support for the effort. And we could see some justification for expanding the theory.

The effectiveness of a planted rumor is well established in the studies of social psychology. I well remember the widespread rumors shortly after Pearl Harbor that had Japanese submarines lurking off the Pacific coast, and the thousands of civilian men armed with hunting rifles and shot guns that swarmed to the beaches to protect us from a sneak invasion. Obviously one of the most effective means, and in many cases the only way we had to imitate such a rumor was by radio communications.

The elements that constitute an effective rumor are that first of all they must be logical and believable. They must have currency and be built around a situation or personage that is generally known. The effect upon the listener must have significance as to his safety, present condition and future prospects. It must suggest a personal reaction either to do something, or at least to mentally prepare him for a future action. The appeal may be emotional or pragmatic. It must be simple and easily translated and may be reduced to a catchword or a phrase that can be simply disseminated. "The Russians are coming!" is an example.

* * * * *

It was about this time, as the Gowen Field school was nearing its end, that I began to wonder, as did a few of "my students," whether we were qualified to conduct any kind of warfare, psychological included. One theory expressed in the after-class bull sessions thought it was merely a classic example of intra-service rivalry between the air force and the army.

A typical expression of my psywarriors was, "I can imagine some top brass at the Air Force Command staff level saying, 'You know, the army has got a monopoly on tactical psywar policy and operations. The air force should not be perceived as just an armed force for actual battle operations, but demonstrate a highly sophisticated capability to wage strategic psywar. We can't let those army bastards look like the only *thinkers* in the Department of Defense!'" This was a rather cynical view by our geniuses, but it did offer to some degree a logical explanation.

It's well to remember that almost all of the persons included in the program were not "military" even though they were in uniform. With the exception of one West Pointer, a half dozen Ph.D.s, and twenty or so M.A.s, the rest of the Georgetown class was made up of brand-new ROTC second lieutenants who had never seen active duty. I was the only company grade officer who had seen combat. There was a small scattering of majors, lieutenant colonels and colonels who were destined to manage the psywar organization and to provide traditional military control of the operational group we were to ultimately become. But the psywar "product" that was to be the result of this effort would be made by novices in the field.

None of us, instructors and students alike, knew what the next assignment would be. It was rumored that some of us would be assigned to various Strategic Air Command (SAC) headquarters units as staffers in their intelligence sections. Another possibility expressed was that we would be members of a unit stationed in the Pentagon as a support to the air force chief of staff. One theory as to assignments, and one I coveted secretly, concerned a position on the staff of The Voice of America or Radio Free Europe. For me, that would have been the frosting on the cake. It's rare that one can apply a military experience to his civilian career. And any assignment in this new psychological warfare field would be an asset in the future.

There was a delay after our temporary duty at psywar school was terminated at Gowen Field, and many of us were scheduled to return to Mountain Home AFB where we had been formally assigned by MATS. Boise was a great city in which to be stationed and housed. Donna and I had found a great basement apartment in one of the many antebellum mansions located on Idaho's capital city's tree-lined streets. It had been a great four-month stay during the early summer of 1952. Our apartment stayed cool day and night, and the lovely surroundings of this city estate with its lawns, trees and gardens allowed for great weekend late afternoon cocktail parties where we entertained our somewhat younger officers and their wives or girl-friends. We were sorry to leave such comfortable and enjoyable sur-roundings, but duty called. And duty in this case was back to Mountain Home AFB where the daily temperatures hovered at the hundred plus mark, and midnight cooled off to perhaps 90 degrees. It was said by regulars that the cowards were volunteering for com-bat overseas!

There were some smaller detachments that were organized for deployment to overseas assignments. One team commanded by a Colonel Arnold was dispatched to an air force command in the Phil-ippines. We learned later that Colonel Arnold had been shot down over Korea on a leaflet drop mission, and had been taken prisoner of war. Arnold was finally released near the end of the war in 1953. Another detachment was dispatched to Algiers, and still I awaited my next orders.

During this standby period the fifty or so of us that marked time were given an I.Q. test that recalled memories still vivid in my mind of exams I'd taken a few years before in flying school that were highly competitive, and that had an immediate effect on one's ca-reer. Here, it wasn't getting "washed out," it was "what's up?"

A minor project was undertaken when the Gowen school had completed its training mission and we were again stationed at Moun-tain Home AFB. I was in charge of a small production unit that was involved in producing leaflets and pamphlets for future dissemination. I had a couple of my bright staffers, including a Major Lay whose father, Bernie Lay, had written a best seller, *God is My Co-Pilot,* and a young Lieutenant Carl Alley who was barely tolerating an interruption to his promising ad agency career in New York City.

We produced a new Civil Defense slogan called "Operation Skywatch," and a logo depicting a young man and woman wearing a white flak helmet as they gazed absently up into the night sky. We submitted it, and Civil Defense liked it, and used it.

Our only other actual operational effort was the organizing, equipping, and staging of an aerial leaflet drop over the city of Walla Walla, Washington. I don't recall the message, but I've often wondered what the citizenry of this small western community thought about this "invasion" of their peaceful environment. I would guess they looked upon us as airborne litterbugs.

It was during my high school senior year that I was first introduced to propaganda. I can recall vividly my indignation when Hubert Armstrong, local Quaker elder, and teacher of my civics class, lectured us on the evils of war. It must be noted that this incident took place in the spring of 1938. Hitler was on the move in Europe and the Japanese were making militant noises in the Far East. There was a vocal growth of isolationism that was emanating with increasing vigor especially from the Middle West. And the local Quaker element was in step with their national and international brethren who were speaking loudly against any war waged by anyone for whatever reason.

Mr. Armstrong started his lecture, I'm tempted to say tirade, with the fervor of an evangelist, which I suppose in a way, he was. His opening salvo was directed at the evil warmongers of WWI, Carnegie and the Du Ponts, and of course the Krepps of Germany. He made no distinction between the Allies and the Huns, the oppressed and the aggressor. And he proceeded to prove his thesis with an 8 mm film of some twenty or so minutes' duration with no disclosure depicted as to the source of the visual material.

The film segments shown were probably actual clips taken during that "Great War to End All Wars." It was graphic, it was brutal, and it was horrifying to the teen age group of rural youngsters whose only exposure to violence was the Saturday matinee at the Bijou when Tom Mix shot the villain.

The film's emphasis was not primarily of life in the trenches which was shown in its grisly reality, but rather a depiction of the atrocities committed by the military; still photographs of sickening brutality committed by men whose uniforms did not clearly identify which side they were on. It was war that made *all men* into unspeakable monsters.

The film showed women, raped and with their arms severed; beheaded children and men, dead, with their limbs detached, lying in blood and gore.

It was truly a shocking experience. A silent group left the classroom when it was over. Some were weeping and everyone was in a state of traumatic shock. Mr. Armstrong dismissed the class without further comment.

The civics class was the last morning class before lunch. I went to my locker, got my lunch box and left for the ranch. I trudged the mile or so to our front driveway gate in a sort of daze. I didn't go in the house and passed unnoticed by anyone on my way down the pasture lane to the swimming hole accompanied by Kim, my Alsatian canine pal.

I sat and stared at the dark water of the peaceful pond and tried to assimilate what I had seen. I knew the pictures were real. I knew war was hell. But I sensed that somehow I had been violated. I knew I would never forget what I had witnessed.

Roy Abner, my dad, was not a profane man. He would utter an occasional damnation, and on rare occasions an SOB. I knew I could not tell my churchgoing mother about the event, but my dad was someone I could confide in. But as I related the day's happening, he exploded. He used words I was familiar with like conscientious objector, isolationist, peace at any price, slacker, pacifist, but each of these was qualified with profane adjectives that I'd never heard before. He was livid with anger.

His initial violent reaction finally cooled somewhat, and with some embarrassment he tried to explain his behavior. His two uncles, one who had fought for the Union army and another who fought for the Confederacy had been killed in the Civil War. He named cousins and classmates who had died fighting for their country in WWI. He quoted Lincoln, Sherman, R. E. Lee, Washington, and Teddy Roosevelt. He reminded me that my own maternal grandfather had stood guard at the White House during the War of 1812. He made the case for our country's history in its involvement and conduct in wars.

What the class of '38 had seen and heard was propaganda. By Armstrong's own definition, it was a deliberate effort on the part of special interest groups to persuade a target audience to accept a point of view that agreed with his group's agenda. The film's producers estimated the attitudinal climate of its audience. They relied on the naiveté of the viewer who had never seen or heard of the subject matter. They exploited the shock effect of the highly inflammatory visual depiction that was so offensive to a largely religious group whose experience left them unprepared to resist the emotional bombardment they had been subjected to. They neglected to distinguish the identity of the *actors*. They did not establish the reliability or credentials of the film's producers. They utilized for authenticity the authority that was implicit in the fact that a respected religious entity presented it as truth.

It was *propaganda,* and it was damned effective. The effects on me were not lasting, not enough to prevent me from volunteering for active service in WWII. But I wonder what emotional residue survived with my other fellow students. It wasn't until I became involved with the psywar program during this Korean War that I could more adequately analyze what I had been exposed to. I was amazed upon reflection how vividly the details of that long ago day's experience came alive, and how easily they were recalled.

A rather sobering conclusion came out of all this. I recognized the effectiveness of propaganda efforts that relied on lies, glittering generalities, sensationalism, and vivid symbolism that could create immediate reactions from a target that would result in riots, lynch-ings, and revolt. But what about the long haul? What about our na-tional character? What about the axiom the truth will out? What would America's credibility be after we had won?

Chapter X

Think Tank

Washington, D.C.'s Rock Creek Park was beautiful this early fall morning. I had to traverse the wooded island that lay between our new residence on 16th Street, The Woodner Apartment hotel complex, and my destination, that familiar illusive address I became acquainted with the first time I was here, 2400 Newark, Headquarters, ARCS (Air Resupply Communications Service).

The day was here now when I would be ordered to try to apply the lessons I had learned at Georgetown University, and Gowen Field, Idaho, that workshop for the application of those lessons. Much to my surprise I had been given a new title that was at the least somewhat intimidating: Chief of the Psychological Warfare Branch.

I hadn't a clue when I finally got this new job as to the details of the assignment. What was the mission of this branch? Who were the people I was to command, and who would implement any product we might create? What sort of "missiles" would we construct? Where would they be aimed? And what results could be expected from successful psywar efforts? Finally, inasmuch as this was still a military operation, what was the chain of command functionally, and what direction would we get from our superiors? Who's on first?

I checked my watch as I entered the large room in the ARCS Headquarters complex that was to be my workplace for the coming months, and it was 0805. I had intended to be a few minutes early and kind of get the lay of the land before anyone else arrived. I was late.

I walked the length of the room to where a group of 15 or 20 young officers were huddled. Someone spotted me approaching and said in a loud voice . . . Tensh-hut! They all turned facing me and stood ramrod straight, in a cadet attention pose.

I damned near fainted.

I managed to keep a stern, straight face and stood for a moment collecting my thoughts, and finally said a few words of greeting.

"Well, this is a dandy way to start the day. You've managed to startle the hell out of me. At ease. Smoke if you've got 'em." With that I walked over to a desk that to my surprise had a nameplate on it that stated this was the property of Captain Alan K. Abner.

I tossed my billed cap with no grommet in it on the desk, turned toward them and sat on the edge.

"If you have seen the table of organization of this outfit you may have noticed there are two majors, a Lieutenant Colonel Murfit, and Colonel Carl Swyter, all of whom are in our ladder of command. You can call *Attention* the first time they enter these hallowed grounds, but I'll bet you'll be told not to do it again. And anyone who does it to me will be lashed."

With that, I grinned at them and asked them to find a seat.

"I'm going to forego my usual sense of modesty and tell you who I am. First of all, I'm one of the few genuine experts in the field of psychological warfare. I've got more hours on the couches of some of this country's leading psychiatrists than anyone in the air force. My essays and treatises on the subject have received countless rejection slips from the American Medical Journal, more than anyone in the field. It was when I overcame a persistent compulsion for stuttering and wetting the bed that I was selected for this assignment."

This, as I hoped, broke the ice, and my audience reacted as I hoped, with laughs and, I suspect, sighs of relief.

"Of course," I continued, "these remarks have been classic propaganda, more commonly known as bull shit. Like you, I enjoyed our recent academic experience at Georgetown. My military background consists of pre-war tour as a corporal in the Oregon National Guard; a four-year hitch as a fighter pilot in the ETO in WWII. As a civilian in the interim before being recalled for this P.W. program I was in commercial radio broadcasting as a newsman and advertising account executive. I also knocked eight strokes off my golf handicap, and perfected the dry martini.

"I hope you, like me, are delighted to be selected to serve in the armed forces in a concept of military activity that involves brains instead of bullets. I'm well aware of the academic credentials each of you brings to this assignment, and I'm confident we can make a significant contribution to winning this Goddamn war, and perhaps even providing some suggestions to aid in winning the peace.

"Except for occasional court-martials I don't expect we'll have a lot of group meetings. Let's take a few days to get acquainted, find out where the good bars and restaurants are, and I'll try to formulate a plan of attack.

"Find a desk, and please remove all heel marks when you leave for the day. And, by the way, I don't need to be reassured by being called Sir except possibly when our top brass is present. I respond amiably to Cap' and react violently to terms like 'Lum' or 'Lil Abner.' I'd appreciate it if you'd all wear your name tags for the notification of next of kin. Carry on."

I stood up and reached out to shake hands with the closest to me, and that started a sort of group movement as each young officer identified himself and exchanged a few words of introduction and greeting. They were a great bunch of guys. They exuded a certain subdued exuberance that I hadn't seen since my old cadet days in flying school. I almost felt ancient by comparison, yet I only exceeded their youth by seven or eight years. I've heard it's not your age but your mileage that counts. At any rate, I still felt contemporary to them, and I viewed my future in this job with relieved enthusiasm.

* * * * *

I had hoped there would be a directive that would define our operational responsibilities and provide some guidance as to what was expected of us, but it soon became apparent that we would have to create our own plan of action. When in doubt, proceed as if you knew what you were doing, and that's what I did.

The academic specialty areas of each member of my group offered some logical reason for specific assignments. Some individuals were designated to serve in a liaison capacity with those elements outside of ARCS with whom we would have to coordinate our efforts: the State Department, The Voice of America, the Army Psychological Tactical Warfare people, Pentagon, Georgetown University's School of Language and Linguistics, and those geographical area experts wherever we found them. Additionally, we would require guidance as to specific areas of possible assistance we might provide to the USAF Strategic Air Command in their ongoing operation in Korea, and our own ARCS operations, wherever they were taking place.

I retained as a sort of "Think Tank" a small group of individuals who demonstrated in different ways special creative talents in addition to their intellectual credentials. Their academic fields ranged from psychology, sociology, economics, English, demography, pre-law, journalism, and even one who planned a graduate career in, of all things, architecture. Their function was to not only create ideas with potential for exploitation, but to develop and finalize plans for presentation to the agency or force that could implement them.

The final form of the completed projects we prepared for presentation to the appropriate recipient followed the familiar military staff study format:
1. statement of the problem
2. factors bearing on the problem
3. recommended action
4. anticipated results

It must be admitted that we made a deliberate effort to "sell" our proposals. We were determined not to be frivolous in our efforts and to seriously research the viability of each plan and be convinced that it was a legitimate, workable enterprise. But we departed somewhat from the sterile style of the typical staff study. We supported the various elements of the study with visual illustrations, graphics and photographs, and packaged the proposals with dramatic covers, usually in color and encased in transparent vinyl that gave it a modern "magazine look." I've no doubt this advertising flak technique caused some negative reaction from some military traditionalists, but we wanted to attract attention to the plan at all levels, and emphasize this wasn't just another product of a bureaucratic paper mill. Perhaps subliminally, we were using psywar techniques in the persuasion of this "friendly" target.

Radio propaganda was of necessity presented in English to be implemented by The Voice of America or Radio Free Europe. They first of all had to determine if our plan was consistent with projects they already had in the works. In many cases we hoped to perhaps just stimulate a new facet of possible action that would fit in with their existing programs. They of course had access to the language and linguistic experts that would translate the messages into the appropriate language, dialect, even jargon, of the target audience. We never presumed to tell these people how or even what to do. They had a long history of highly effective discourse with their "audience," and we were amateurs in their field.

The last category in which we were interested was the area of Warfare Psychologically Waged. These proposals involved recommended policies or actions by both air and ground force planners in aspects other than typical military operations. This was for situations that did not involve leaflet drops or radio communications, but rather devices that could be utilized to influence the techniques used in the interrogation of prisoners; the handling of civilians in newly occupied specific areas by our forces; the establishment of rumors within the enemy's military and civilian populations, and suggested techniques for demoralizing the morale of enemy troops.

In all of our efforts we took great care not to presume, to criticize, or imply any attitude of superiority over the long-established military intelligence departments we had to deal with, and upon whom we would depend for implementation. The product that emerged from our "Tank" was no doubt unconventional and viewed by some, I suppose, as radical, but it was always based on sound behavioral theories.

We never got any criticism from our superiors. If they were receiving any negative feedback from any source they didn't burden us with it. Perhaps they did not want to dampen our enthusiasm, but I had never found *that* consideration to be a factor in hearing from my superiors if they were unhappy with anything.

We rarely heard back on the fate of any of our submitted projects, but we "muddled on," as the British say.

* * * * *

All of the members of the psywar division in ARCS had Top Secret Security clearances. The granting of these qualifications required complete investigations of the individual backgrounds of the subject officers that involved visits by FBI agents to the home towns of each. I can imagine the reaction of the agent sent to Newberg, Oregon, my home, if he interviewed my grammar school truant officer. "Oh yeah," he might say. "I remember that Abner kid. He lived on a ranch a couple of miles out of town, and he might detour on his way to school to hitchhike to Portland, 26 miles away, or even to the coast which was 150 miles round-trip. We rarely caught him. He slowed down a little when he got to high school."

Apparently my early tendency to travel did not constitute a threat to national security, because I was cleared. The rest of my Think Tank gang probably had slight blemishes on their early records also, but they were all outstanding young men. They were bright, dedicated, and were indeed the cream of our nation's 1951 college graduates. They were all eager to contribute to our war effort in this relatively new field for the air force, psychological warfare. But like me, they were somewhat intimidated by a rather obscure mission whose goals were not clearly defined, and the results of the *missions* we submitted were never disclosed to us.

The factors that determined the selection of our targets came from many sources, but they all started with the dominant theme that our ultimate target was the USSR, and the desired results of our effort were to damage our real enemy's activities in the waging of its proxy war in Korea.

Some of our projects originated in proposals submitted by economics people who found "bread and butter" elements in areas within the Soviet bloc. In others, psychologists and sociologists found not so latent attitudes based on religious and cultural suppressions. Historic and ethnic grievances lay smoldering in many areas with long-standing hatreds. Area experts revealed difficulties experienced by the communist invaders in solving the language problems, the unique social mores of the citizens, and finally, the most significant of all, the massive frustration in all of the occupied countries of being held captive, and without freedom.

Each area we probed had a dominant field for psywar exploitation, though they all had many of the same vulnerabilities in common. Poland for example, had a long history of conflicts with its neighbor to the East. They had recently been attacked by the Nazis and betrayed by the Russians in WWII. The youth of this beleaguered country did not have to read history or hear war stories from their elders to know current hatred.

Czechoslovakia was a similar situation. Yugoslavia was a mishmash of clannish geographic and religious subdivisions held together for one of the few times in its chaotic history by Joseph Broz Tito, a Communist dictator with his own communist theory who remained a rebellious thorn in the side of the Kremlin.

The Ukraine is a soviet republic with a long history of independence, a country rich in natural resources and a bread basket for the Soviet armed forces as well as the rest of Russia. This subdued society, along with others in the soviet orbit like Azerbaijan, Byelorussia, Lithuania, Armenia, and of course the Baltic States, all had potent subliminal vulnerabilities for psywar.

Among our first *targets* was Poland with its obvious receptivity as a strong Catholic populace, and its historic resistance to Russia. Another vulnerable area was Romania which was chosen for a number of sound academic reasons, but mainly selected for its being a principal source of petroleum products for the Russian air force. Ploesti had been a prime target in WWII, and its importance to the military operations of the Soviet in both Russia and Korea was very significant.

The manner in which the various psywar operational efforts were to be delivered to the target *audience* involved consideration of various factors:

1. Was the physical location of the target rural or urban?

2. Was the operation to be conducted during the day or night?

3. Did the target exist in a specific area such as a factory, a troop concentration, a strategic rail or highway center, or a particularly depressed region?

4. Was there an active resistant group such as the deadly French Maquis of WWII?

5. What were the current weather conditions?

6. What penalties would be enforced by the Communists if a partisan was caught?

7. Was there an existing escape mechanism in place for defectors to flee to the West?

8. Did propaganda or subversive materials known to be from the United States have acceptance as to America's credibility?

The various materials used in implementing the goal of the operation covered a wide range:

1. Aerial drops of leaflets that depicted propaganda; maps, cartoons, news, photographs, etc.

2. Radio broadcasts disseminated by The Voice of America, Radio Free Europe, and clandestine short-wave transmitters

3. Rumors initiated by an underground that was stimulated by word of mouth by agents

4. A variety of rather gimmicky items such as parcels of Bull Durham type packets of tobacco with cigarette papers, each with a message

5. Toilet paper with illustrated sheets with catch words, mottos, slogans, etc.

6. Small cigarette pack size AM radio receivers

7. A limited distribution of shock-proof short-wave transmitters

8. Carefully distributed explosives to select targets

It should come as no surprise that my staff of young enthusiasts would come up with some outrageous proposals designed to frustrate or enrage the enemy.

One idea at first glance was hilarious by its absurdity, but as the author of the plan argued, it had the endorsement of England's war time prime minister, Winston Churchill.

It seemed that after the British defeat in Norway in March 1940, it was suggested to the First Lord of the Admiralty that rubber sheaths be issued to the Royal Marines to protect the $10^1/_2$-inch barrels of their rifles from sweating, then freezing, in the Arctic temperatures.

Churchill examined a test box of the condoms from the pharmaceutical company and promptly rejected it. When asked why, he responded that "there was no labeling on the box or the packets it contained."

His rather ribald reasoning was explained.

"I want a label for every box, every carton, every packet, saying 'British-Size Medium.' That will show the Nazis, if they ever obtain one of them, who's the master race!"

Our more conservative "editors" reluctantly rejected the proposal, thinking it might be offensive to our own constituency if it became a tabloid headline.

* * * * *

"I came from a broken home. My mother was a Republican and my father was a Democrat." This was a line I had used on a few occasions when I had introduced a political candidate for local or state office in Oregon, and a couple of times when I was called upon to speak at Rotary or other service clubs.

My own political posture was somewhat ambiguous. I was a registered Democrat principally out of loyalty to my dad who was a

Jeffersonian Democrat, and though he came from a Midwestern conservative clan of doctors, and was a graduate pharmacist himself, he was a rancher at heart, and FDR's New Deal had saved our ranch and our skin during the Great Depression. I had some vivid recollections of those terrible times when our dairy produced less than 30 dollars a week in cash, and my older brother Paul had gone to work for the WPA, driving a truck to supplement our existence.

My mother was a quietly determined Republican who was equally thankful for what FDR had done in those bleak depression years, and more recently, winning the great war. "But they are so mean about poor Mr. Hoover," she would say. "Everyone forgets what great humanitarian work he did as administrator of our Relief Program for Europe After WWI."

Additionally, we all were reminded almost daily that Hoover, a Quaker, had spent a good deal of his youth attending Newberg's George Fox Academy, a local Quaker prep school. A beautiful sign (erected by the DAR) attached to an ancient oak tree overlooking a large pond of Chehalem Creek that ran through our pastures proclaimed this site was "The Boyhood Swimming Hole of Herbert Hoover."

I do not want to give the impression that Sylvia Abner was a docile rural housewife. She had earned a teacher's certificate at Washington State's Normal school at Pullman and had taught elementary school before her marriage to Roy Abner. She was not loathe to argue for her political point of view, and she was an active participant in the nightly political conversations that were never antagonistic but certainly forceful by all parties, including me, the youngest by nine years.

So, it's apparent that I was something of a political hybrid, a social democrat, and at the same time a fiscal conservative. Roosevelt was the only president I knew with any clarity. He was my commander in chief in WWII, and I recall that rainy night in England, huddled around a pot-bellied stove with my mates listening to "Berlin Calling," the nightly Nazi propaganda broadcast that knew our names. Ironically, it was here that I learned from a gleeful Lord Haw Haw that our president was dead. I cried for him, though I unexplainably hadn't and didn't for comrades lost in combat.

1952 was an election campaign year, and though our psywar group was engrossed in getting our operation productive we all were very interested in the *psychological warfare* being waged by the two political parties fighting for the presidency.

I had no idea as to the political affiliations of my team members. If I had been so inclined, I'm sure I could have made some more or less intelligent guesses as to their party choices. The young second lieutenants with B.A. degrees in liberal arts leaned toward the Democrats, and their candidate, Adlai Stevenson. The Ivy League grads were inclined to be more conservative and favored Republican Dwight Eisenhower. Though in our after-hours discussions about the campaigns, rarely did anyone couch their observations in partisan terms. Rather, it was a *professional* analysis of the techniques and devices employed by both parties.

Stevenson was labeled an "Egg Head," a slur that irritated his supporters, who were rather secretly smug in having him as one of them, *true intellectuals.* He was called a dreamer, a theorist who spoke a language no one could understand. One extremist columnist even called him a "Parlor Pink"; another, a "Lace Curtain Liberal."

Republican Eisenhower presented a difficult problem for the Democrat campaign strategists. First of all, he was still a national hero of gargantuan proportions. His *Crusade in Europe* was a best seller. He was an extremely popular civilian with a grin that was the envy of Madison Avenue hucksters and Hollywood agents. He came from Kansas, for God's sake. Born in Abilene. How American can you get? He had gained some intellectual stature by serving as president of Columbia University. And finally in the closing days of the race, he played his wartime five star general chip, and declared "he would go to Korea."

The Stevenson speech writers and campaign planners could not attack this hero. They weakly reminded the uninterested electorate that Civil War general Grant had been a disaster as the chief executive. General Washington remained unscathed. And the best they could do was to invoke the memory of Herbert Hoover, the "architect of the Great Depression."

This wasn't fertile ground for a Democrat psywarrior. There was no great sea of discontent in a country that was flushed with postwar prosperity. There were few fractious factions that could be incited to get active in their opposition to Eisenhower. There were no scandals to uncover. The candidate had a story book marriage and family, and his personal behavior was impeccable. He was impregnable.

But the parallel between warfare psychologically waged and political campaigns was fascinating. Many of the devices used to influence people's attitudes, and hopefully ultimate voting behavior, were used by both factions. But there were no vicious attacks such as those that characterized Abraham Lincoln's re-election campaign almost a century before. Besides, "the Democrats have been in long enough. It's time for a change."

But the coup de grace was the political slogan that was probably the best one ever coined:

"I like Ike."

* * * * *

There was no confusion in our ranks as to the identity of the enemy. Though our foe on the battlefield was communist North Korea, the real enemy was the USSR. The army's psywar efforts were aimed at troops on the ground, and the surrounding citizenry. Our strategic goal, as we defined it, was to create disaffection in one form or another with the Russian support structure.

The nature of the USSR's totalitarian form of government offered fertile grounds for exploitation. Within the boundaries of the greater Soviet Union were the "annexed" republics such as the Ukraine, Byelorussia, Azerbaijan, Armenia, Georgia, Uzbek, etc. One hundred sixty-nine different ethnic groups were represented in the sphere of soviet control. Many of these groups had independent histories with renewed traditions, religious beliefs, customs, and ancient resentments of exploitation by their more powerful neighbors, including czarist Russia and the recent USSR.

Outside the perimeter of the USSR, a series of "treaties" from in 1943 through 1948 between the Soviet Union and eight eastern European countries widened the territory behind the Iron Curtain: Czechoslovakia, Yugoslavia, Albania, Poland, Rumania, Hungary, Bulgaria, and Finland. East Germany, established by the Russians in 1949, was also included. One obvious chink in the alliance was Yugoslavia where Marshall Tito proved noncooperative, and soviet policy was one of hostility to his regime.

All of these areas under soviet control had latent elements that provided opportunities for exploitation: Poland, Czechoslovakia, Yugoslavia, the Baltic nations because of their strategic location, certain provinces in greater Russia such as the Ukraine, and last but not least, China with its long history of conflict with its bordering communist big brother. These areas were particularly potent, and we gave them high priority as possible targets.

Chapter XI
$10,000 Mig

The selection of a psywar target area required detailed analysis and coordination with factors related to not only our current military situations, but also the positioning of the United States with its Allies, and its image worldwide with other nations not directly involved in the Korean conflict. The dissemination of propaganda was practiced widely by many governments throughout the world, and even the most unsophisticated recipient of these efforts viewed most of the messages with some skepticism. To have any impact we knew our efforts must be well disguised and have not only credibility but high emotional appeal. In one instance we violated at least one of our own rules but presented a rather novel plan anyway.

Intelligence reports indicated a degree of dissatisfaction existed in the USSR's armed forces within the Russian air force in the more conservative, traditional members of the army, navy and special forces. The Russian top command was made up of older career army officers who viewed this *new* military arm as a threat to their long-established supremacy in waging conventional warfare. The younger commanding officers in the air force were constantly frustrated in their efforts to take what they considered to be their proper role in the scheme of things. Their views were shared by the pilots themselves, who, though they considered themselves the elite of the military establishment, felt they were not respected or even utilized to their greatest potential by the gray beards at the top. There had been a few desertions by these disgruntled pilots, and we felt there was a potential for additional defections if properly motivated.

Our plan called for the offer of a $10,000 reward for a Mig, a Russian jet, and asylum for the pilot delivering the aircraft to Allied territory.

The plan was classified Top Secret, and great emphasis was placed on the requirement that the offer not be given any attributable publicity that would indicate the offer was official policy by the U.S. Air Force or our federal government. Rather, it was essential that information about the reward was to be disseminated by word-of-mouth through the ranks of the enemy military in the Korean War zone.

We did not expect any reaction from the Russian pilots in the actual theater of operations as they were too closely supervised in their tactical role to have an opportunity to defect. Rather, we expected that the response would come on Russia's western borders where escape would be much easier to Allied airfields in West Germany, France, etc.

We realized that the Soviets would create an outraged protest in reaction to this plan before the United Nations if they could prove that the United States was attempting to bribe innocent, naive soldiers to betray their country. Our U.N. ambassador would have a certain advantage of deniability if the plan were implemented in a covert fashion, as we explained in great detail.

We forwarded the plan to the Pentagon on a Monday. We didn't expect any immediate reaction, as we often never learned whether our psywar plans were adopted, or whether they were effective when implemented. On the following Saturday, however, I was shocked by the headlines of the *Washington Post* that greeted me as I approached a newsstand at the entrance of our apartment building.

GEN. MARK CLARK OFFERS $100,000 REWARD FOR RUSSIAN JET.

I bought a couple of copies of the *Post*, made my way down to the basement garage where our Roadmaster was parked, put the convertible top down, and drove out into the brilliant sunshine of a beautiful early spring morning. By the time I reached the Newark Street Headquarters, I had sorted out my reaction to this startling event. I assumed my young staff of psywar "experts" would be shocked, angry, alarmed, indignant, rebellious, etc.

I was wrong. They were highly amused in a rather sardonic way. As I entered the work area, the whole congregation went silent for just an instant, then all hell broke loose.

"Hey Cap,' we have finally arrived. General Mark Clark really likes our fiendish plot. He wants a Russian Mig and he's willing to pay for it. I guess he doesn't know we've already got a couple of those jets."

"Gee, I'm really sorry the *Post* didn't credit us with the idea. The Georgetown folks would have been quietly proud if they had."

"I wonder how much General Clark would give for a tank? If this idea really works we could create a helluva War Surplus materiels business."

"Well, one thing's for sure. When we put a TOP SECRET classification on a project, they know we mean business!"

I was relieved that this lighthearted raillery was the mood of the moment, but I knew that behind the facades of carefully disguised ridicule was a feeling of disappointment and some disillusionment with the way our proposal had been distorted.

Gradually the more or less good-natured comments died down, and except for the shaking of a few heads in disbelief, and a cuss word or two, the staff settled down at their desks and looked a little nervously at me. I knew it was no time for humor, and no bull shit about "ours is not to wonder why," and other military axioms.

"I've just gained a new understanding about how our commander in chief, President Truman, must have felt when General Douglas MacArthur disregarded his direct orders and policy positions, and went public with his own theories about how to wage the war. Well, that general got fired. Lincoln had the same problems with McClellan, Churchill with Montgomery, and I suppose Caesar with Mark Antony. It usually happens when the egos of otherwise competent high ranking individuals overpower their judgment. So it would appear that our momentary irritation with General Clark has plenty of precedence.

The day Yeager shot down five ME-109s

"Something it might be well to consider is the fact that a lot of very bright people up through the chain of command thought our plan had merit and that it deserved doing. They are probably as pissed off as we are. But they'll 'muddle through,' as our British friends say, and so will we.

"It just occurred to me that today is Saturday, and I've got a starting time at the Army Navy Country Club at 12:30. I feel like knocking the Hell out of something, so it might as well be a golf ball. And a social note. Eddie Heywood is doing a gig tonight at the Blue Mirror—you may know the joint across from the Ambassador Hotel downtown—and if any of you jazz buffs drop in, I'll buy you one. Repeat. One."

* * * * *

It was some thirty years later that I was to finally learn the fate of the $100,000 Mig Jet offer. The confirmation of our "bribe" was revealed in the publication of the book *Yeager*, an autobiography by Chuck Yeager, published by Bantam Books in 1985.

This book that recounted in vast detail the career of this out-standing pilot from WWII to date brought back a flood of memories from that combat against the German Luftwaffe in 1944–45.

Lieutenant John Casey, a long-time best-buddy since flying school, and I were in the pilot's lounge (a Quonset hut with a bar) one night after Yeager had rejoined the 363rd Fighter Squadron, 357th Fighter Group in England, 1944.

Flight Officer Yeager had been shot down on his eighth mission on May 5, 1944, the day after he had scored his first air victory shoot-ing down an ME-109 fighter. He had parachuted safely and though injured walked out of enemy territory to Switzerland. Some three months later he appeared before General Dwight Eisenhower at SHAEF Headquarters in London to gain special approval to rejoin his group in combat. Ike approved, and here he was to tell about it.

Both Casey and I were impressed by this young, confident, al-most cocky junior officer. It was no surprise to any of us that he would make his own mark in a group that boasted more than 20 aces. He had all the qualities. A superlative pilot, a born engineer, and like Bud Anderson he had the eyes of an eagle. They both could spot a "bogey" miles before anyone else.

His aggressive leadership abilities within weeks after his return had him leading his squadron on occasions, and eventually he was commanding group escort missions as lieutenant. It was on such a mission on October 12, 1945, to Bremen that, as the lead plane, he spotted a gaggle of enemy fighters and shot down five aircraft, making him an ace in one mission. His squadron claimed a total of eight victories and Yeager was awarded the Silver Star.

After V.E. Day in 1945 1 had followed Chuck Yeager's career with great interest as he became in peace time the number one test pilot in the air force. On October 14, 1947, he was the first pilot to break the sound barrier, something many thought could never be done.

The book, though it recalled many events from those days of combat over Europe, made a revealing leap to the war we were waging in Korea. At the peak of his career as a top test pilot for the air force here is Yeager's account of an occasion that was for me a most satisfying event.

Yeager recalls being on the Kadena Air Force Base, Okinawa, February 1954: "Here I was standing on the wing of a Russian-built Mig fighter . . . a Mig 15." The assignment was to test fly the aircraft to determine its capabilities against our Sabre jet fighters which were facing them over Korea. Yeager and another USAF test pilot had been brought to the middle of the Pacific Ocean because a North Korean pilot named Kim Sok Ho had defected in his Mig 15. He had received $100,000 reward and asylum.

I had always felt a vicarious pride in the career of one of our old 363rd Fighter Squadron alumni. Now, I was additionally gratified to belatedly learn the successful results of the "Georgetown Whiz Kids" $10,000 reward plan.

Chapter XII
"Big Mac"

"I've got a little chore for you guys," Colonel Swyter said. We were a little surprised at the colonel's statement because this was the first time in the months we had been cranking out P.W. materials that we'd had any reaction from the people over us in the ARCS command. We all enjoyed this apparent absence of supervision or direction, though we did sometimes wonder whether the product we were turning out was being utilized operationally. I wondered what this "chore" would be that Colonel Swyter had in mind.

I'd had a call earlier that Friday afternoon from Swyter who asked me to select a couple of my best writers to meet with us after the rest of the staff had left for the day. Wow! Maybe this was a real clandestine assignment that would present a new exciting challenge. I had picked Bill Blatty first for obvious reasons in that he was the best scribe of us all. Claire Rubley, Dave Wheelwright, and Steve Adams, who in addition to making the best martinis in the air force, brought a quiet dignity and Southern charm to his work that reflected the social, cultural, and literary background he'd been raised with in North Carolina.

"We're getting a new ARCS commander," Swyter continued. "He's a brigadier general who comes to us from his recent tour as a U.S. Air Attaché in Paris. He saw combat as a pilot in twin-engine aircraft in WWII in North Africa and Italy, and I believe he was on the Ploesti raids. He's new to MATS and I suspect he's not too knowledgeable about the ARCS mission, and probably not up to speed on our psywar division.

"We have been requested to prepare a draft of a speech he will give at a reception for all ARCS staff members next Tuesday. He arrives here to take command next Monday morning at 1100 and, Captain Abner, you and I will escort him here from Andrews AFB at that time." Our boss paused and lighted a cigarette.

"Well, there it is," Carl concluded. "I'm not going to advise you on how to write it. I know it's short notice but use whatever means you have to get it right. There will be no editorial oversight. The general instructed me to maintain a FYEO (for your eyes only) security on it. I'll see the final draft and that's it. OK. Damn the torpedoes, full speed ahead."

I sat in the front seat with the driver of the command car staring straight ahead poised to respond to any question that might come from the back seat. No sounds came from behind me except for the rustling of paper as General Monroe McCloskey read our speech. He had been unsmiling but correct as we greeted him upon his arrival at Andrews AFB, and his only response to Colonel Swyter's inquiry about his trip was to comment tersely that it was "satisfactory." He took the black plastic leatherette foldex that Carl offered him as we approached the vehicle and after getting seated, proceeded to read our "Top Secret Project."

General McCloskey reminded me of someone, and I couldn't quite put my finger on it. He was tall and very erect. He was obviously in pretty good shape, and his tanned face was rather gaunt with a prominent, slightly hooked nose that gave him a rather arrogant air. His voice was hoarse, slightly guttural and flat, void of much inflection though he'd not spoken a half dozen words since our meeting.

Suddenly, it came to me. He was a dead ringer for a young Douglas MacArthur. Not only did he resemble the recently deposed commander of our forces in Korea, but he acted like "Mac." He had that same attitude that somehow he was above the crowd. He had that same photogenic trick of pausing and looking at a distant vision as if seeking divine intervention. I don't know why I got these impressions during this rather brief exposure to the man, but later demonstrations of his command style generally confirmed that sometimes first reactions to someone are correct. Carl apparently had the same ideas as mine which he later summed up succinctly . . . "The general at least doesn't smoke a corncob pipe."

* * * * *

I'm not sure that my curiosity about General McCloskey was purely academic. I may have been stimulated by his appearance at a reception held in his honor shortly after his taking command of ARCS. This occasion was staged to acquaint the entire officer staff and their wives with their new commanding officer. The early evening affair was formal and the ladies wore gowns and their best accessories. The men were dressed in their blue class A uniforms with awards and decorations bravely displayed. The general made a slightly delayed appearance resplendent in an All White Dress Uniform that many of us had never seen before or even knew existed. There was no confusion as to who was the star of this production.

There's no doubt that the general's uniform was "regulation." And it possibly was correct and appropriate at the diplomatic levels he was accustomed to during his tenure as an air attaché in Paris. But it seemed to me to make the event not a get-together of a wartime military unit with their leader, but rather a sort of coronation.

I'd met just one general in my own military career. That was Major General Jimmy Doolittle, famous air force hero, when he greeted us newly arrived replacement pilots to his combat command in Cambridge, England, in 1944. He wore an issue Eisenhower jacket.

I hesitated to "analyze" General McCloskey. Perhaps it was because at that time we were analyzing everything! But I couldn't resist looking for comparisons in the impact of the personalities of leaders in command on those subordinates that are then inspired to follow and to serve them. My first impression of McCloskey was one of cautious respect because of his almost theatrical demeanor and formal bearing. His recital almost word for word of our prepared script indicated an agile mind and no lack of mental acuity.

He was undoubtedly intelligent and well educated. His cool treatment of Colonel Swyter, however, upon his arrival, indicated no interest or recognition of the rows of decorations displayed by the senior combat-seasoned officer and showing the eagles rank which the one star general had just recently vacated. There was no fraternal warmth of one old campaigner toward another obvious equal, if not in rank, certainly in past performances under fire.

I was intrigued but not sure it signified anything.

Chapter XIII

This Is the Army

The theory expressed at one point by one of our Whiz kids regarding the reason the air force had initiated our psywar program was that it was imperative that the army not be the exclusive branch in the Department of Defense that had an arsenal that contained brains as well as bullets. The army's *tactical* psywar operations were designed to function in the actual combat arena, and obviously were reasonably effective in bombarding troops on the ground with leaflets and aerial loudspeakers aimed at encouraging defection and generally undermining morale. These devices were also useful in warning civilian targets of impending operations by air or on the ground, urging the inhabitants to evacuate or to take cover. We of course applauded these efforts but felt there was a legitimate military and civilian target to be exploited that was *strategic* in its goals.

I, and the other members of the ARCS psywar division felt no feelings of rah-rah competition with the army guys and their program. But we had heard that at the more lofty levels within the Department of Defense existed an aura of irritation between some air force and army brass that threatened to create a more substantial climate for verbal conflict.

Colonel Carl Swyter made me aware of this internal situation and told me of an assignment he and I would undertake to alleviate some of these tensions that could become a minor problem between the two military branches.

A meeting had been scheduled where we were to meet with our army psywar counterparts in the Pentagon. Carl assured me that it wasn't necessary for me to prepare any sort of an elaborate briefing presentation. Rather, this get-together would be informal in nature, and the topics to be discussed would be confined to a general description of our activities more in a philosophical vein than specific operational efforts. I was somewhat intimidated at the prospect, but at the same time relieved that I needn't get my crew distracted from projects we were developing.

I left our digs at the Woodner a few minutes earlier than usual and wheeled the Buick four-holer with the top down through Rock Creek Park, enjoying a beautiful spring morning en route to our headquarters on Newark Street. I hoped this was a good sign that the rest of the day would be equally pleasant. I arrived a few minutes early at the work place and was somewhat amused at the staff, who though they looked rather startled at seeing me in my Class A dress uniform, ribbons and all, refrained from any smart-ass asides. They knew something was up, but the "need-to-know" security rule was in place and no one violated it.

Even though the colonel had told me there was no need for any visual materials for the conference, I still felt unarmed for combat and put a copy of one of our flashiest projects in a new black leather zippered legal size envelope along with a folded map of Europe and Asia that included the Korean Theater. At the last minute I added a yellow lined legal pad and a couple of pencils though I doubted any notes would be taken.

At 0900 Colonel Swyter arrived and I must say his entrance certainly topped mine. He too was in full Class A dress from his cap visored with scrambled eggs and a chest decorated with four rows of ribbons on the left side topped by Command Pilot wings, and a couple of framed decorations on the right. I damned near called "Attention" myself, but he had made it clear early on that he didn't require it.

The colonel smiled broadly at the staff all standing at their desks facing him and waved to them, signaling his appreciation. I quickly gathered up my cap and briefing folder and headed toward where he was waiting at the door, pausing only to hand Lieutenant Blatty a folded piece of paper that had the phone number on it where I could be reached in an emergency. I learned later that he had quickly determined that it was a Pentagon extension. So much for "need to know."

There was no conversation as we were driven to our appointment. The colonel made no comment as the staff car driver found a route that turned on 23rd Street, headed across town around the Lincoln Memorial, across the Arlington Bridge, and then left toward our destination. Neither of us commented on the beauty of the cherry blossoms we had passed on the routes, but the sight of an airliner in a landing mode for the Washington International Airport caused Carl to say, "It's great flying weather." I agreed.

The driver proceeded unerringly to the entrance indicated on his trip slip; the security guys quickly scrutinized and approved the paper Colonel Swyter gave to them; we accepted and hung a plastic badge on our blouses and departed into the ominous structure as the colonel informed the guard that he knew where our appointment office was located.

"I served time in this fortress some years ago," Carl said. I was somewhat amused at his use of the phrase "served time," but I couldn't argue with the use of a convict's jargon. Barred walls do a prison make.

Our heels clicked smartly on the mile or so of the hard-surfaced hallway floors and finally we came to a double door entry with a uniformed guard on duty in front. My "guide" glanced at the number on the door, and without changing our pace we proceeded down the corridor a block or so to an intersection where we paused as the colonel glanced at his watch.

We stood there for perhaps four or five minutes. Finally, with another glance at his watch, my "guide," without a word, led me back to the entry we had passed, handed a paper to the guard who immediately rapped twice on the door, opened it, and stood at attention, holding it open with his extended right arm. I glanced at my watch. The second hand read 60 as the minute hand arrived at 1000. Wow! We were over the target.

* * * * *

It might be appropriate here to discuss Colonel Carl Swyter. I had a great personal relationship with Carl. Perhaps partially because he had started his military career in the U.S. Army Air Corps as a pursuit pilot, and I was the only one in our outfit also a fighter jock. He was "Carl" when we went through the Georgetown psywar graduate courses. We generally sat side by side in classes and seminars, and after hours Donna and I socialized with Carl and his beautiful English wife, Peggy, regularly. We played golf together most weekends, and the four of us spent weekends at Williamsburg and the Pinehurst golf resort. We spent a lot of time after duty hours in "civvies" and he was "Carl."

This day was one of the rare times I had been with him in a formal military environment. And today he was a *Bird Colonel*!

I followed him into the meeting room a couple of paces behind and removed my cap as he did. He paused after a few steps, and stood surveying the room. A couple of windows faced us on the opposite wall with the mid-morning sun streaming into the rather small room, illuminating a rectangular table about ten feet long with four chairs on each side and one on each end. To our left, standing stiffly, were a lieutenant colonel, a major, a captain, and a master sergeant, all in Army Class A uniforms.

"Good morning, Colonel," the lieutenant colonel said, and then identified himself and the two officers with him.

"Good morning," my boss replied. "And my associate is Captain Abner. Does the sergeant have a name?" he asked with a sort of frosty smile.

The lieutenant colonel reddened slightly and offered the sergeant's name who was standing by a small table at the wall to our left where a square black box, obviously a tape recorder, was displayed along with a coffee pot that rested on a warmer, and two mugs. The "Sarge" was the only one to display a large friendly grin.

"My name is Swyter," Carl said. "With a Y," he concluded. He then sort of stared at the group still standing at the end of the table. They had obviously been early for the meeting. The lieutenant colonel stood at the end of the table and his two associates were to his left with their backs to the windows. Each officer had a pad, a coffee cup, and an ashtray that emitted slight whiffs of smoke from cigarettes that smoldered there.

The colonel (Carl, of course) moved to our right, placing his cap on the table, motioned me to a seat to his right and seated himself at the end chair facing the army guys some ten feet away. Now my back was to the windows.

It was immediately apparent who was the ranking officer for this *informal* chat. It was obvious to me that this was a classic example of military "gamesmanship." If Carl had accepted the seating arrangement as it was when he entered, he would be in the side chair opposite the major and the captain with the army lieutenant colonel at the head of the table, the presiding position.

The lieutenant colonel, still slightly pink, recovered quite nicely.

"Would you care for some coffee, Colonel Swyter?" he asked. "And you too, of course, Captain Abner." Not waiting for an answer, he turned and nodded to the "Sarge" who quickly complied. With that, he picked up his coffee cup, leaving his pad and cigarette, and moved smoothly down the table to the chair on Carl's left and motioned his *staff* to seats down the table next to me. Now he was the only one with the sun in his face. From a fighter pilot's point of view, that was just right.

Colonel Swyter led off the session on a light note by complimenting the army officer's attire. He recalled with a slight inflection of nostalgia that he had worn the forest green blouse and pink pants for over twenty years in the now extinct Army Air Corps, and still regarded that uniform as one of the best of military garb in the world. I certainly shared that view.

A brief description of MATS, the Military Air Transport Service, followed in a brief, but a more detailed general analysis of our outfit, ARCS, the Air Resupply and Communications Service, and defined the traditional mission of ARCS in supporting ground elements, civilian and military, with a wide variety of materials. He explained the logic reasoned by the air force and the Defense Department in creating our psywar operations to supplement the army's *tactical* psychological warfare efforts with our mission to support *strategic* military plans with a psywar overlay. He carefully lauded the army's activities in their specialized area.

The army lieutenant colonel responded with a generalized description of the ground forces psywar mission with some emphasis on the history of their existence which preceded ours by several years, and apparently more than one war.

Neither spokesman described any TOP SECRET details of their operations. The only exception that came close was Swyter's description of situations that could require close coordination between the two forces in the dissemination of psywar campaign materials or messages. He referred to our $10,000 reward offer for a Russian Mig jet aircraft that became *public information,* and remarked that it had been our emphasized intention that the offer be made by word-of-mouth at the theater ground level. This, he explained, gave the U.S. diplomatic level an excuse to deny knowledge of the "bribe" in the United Nations assembly and in the world press.

Colonel Swyter's message was clear. He didn't need to name General Mark Clark as the culprit. Neither did he at any time refer to the army's top icon, General Douglas MacArthur, and his recent firing by President Truman.

I couldn't help but wonder whether the tape recording that had been documenting the session, operated by the sergeant, would be edited before release to the higher level army command. I hoped our copy of the tape to our superiors would be intact.

The meeting lasted about an hour. It was an apparently cordial get-together; it was *correct,* and it probably didn't change anyone's mind or alter any prejudices or rivalries. It reminded me of what might have been a corporate board meeting where one of the board's members was secretly planning a stock takeover.

*   *   *   *   *

"That's the third time I've been in the Pentagon, Colonel, and I'm sure glad our operation was assigned the Newark Street facilities. The Fortress, as you so aptly called it, really gives me the willies."

"I spent two years there one summer a while back," Carl said. "That's a joke, Son." He smiled and glanced at the driver who showed no interest in our conversation.

"'The Wild Blue Yonder' it ain't. But it sure as hell dramatizes the contrast between a combat unit overseas and an assignment at a high command staff level in that environment," I said.

"Well, that's true enough," he agreed. "But at the same time that awesome structure becomes a constant reminder of the vast scope of the military's responsibilities during war times, and in a strange way you are actually inspired to match your performance to the larger mission."

We didn't engage in any review of our meeting with the U.S. Army folks. I told him that I thought it had gone well, and that I hoped his reference to General Mark Clark had not gone unnoticed. His only response was that perhaps we had opened a door to further efforts to coordinate our operations in the future . . . but he doubted it.

"Those people are a helluva lot more involved in sophisticated psywar than just dropping leaflets on ground troops. They did some pretty interesting things in WWII with motion pictures that they didn't discuss today. I suspect our stuff may be pretty much in the embryonic stage."

When I returned to work that day I didn't feel that the events of the afternoon were significant enough to brief the staff, but later after duty hours, I did discuss the matter with Lieutenant Blatty who had lingered out of curiosity after the others had gone for the day. I gave him a pretty complete account of the meeting (it was not a classified event) with emphasis on Colonel Swyter's final observation to me about the army's capabilities and history in the area of motion pictures as a key psywar device.

I was well aware of this junior officer's keen intellect and his demonstrated superiority as our best scribe. It was some years later as Blatty gained national attention as a writer that I recalled his remarks that day and his recognition of the value of film-making as perhaps the major contributor in the wars to win men's minds.

The Exorcist, William Blatty's sensational novel published in 1971 was dubbed "The Shocker of the Year." In the following months Harper and Row Publishers issued 13 hard cover printings, and the Bantam edition 12 paper back printings. The reviews were raves and widespread. The *New York Times* said, "*The Exorcist* is as superior to most books of its kind as an Einstein equation is to an accountant's column of figures."

I was not surprised at Second Lieutenant Blatty's ultimate literary success. He was by far the most effective officer of all of my Think Tank psywar operatives, and I recall our mutual interest in motion pictures as not only an intriguing entertainment diversion, but as a future civilian career possibility. He successfully went on to excel not only in writing best sellers, but to see his creative works produced on film.

At the time I did not realize the huge deficiency in our psywar propaganda program was our lack of emphasis on motion pictures, or a capability to utilize this medium in our arsenal.

This retrospect caused me to realize that I was rather negligent in my appraisal of the army's long interest and involvement in the production of motion pictures, particularly in WWII. I did some research.

* * * * *

George Creel at the behest of then-President Woodrow Wilson was finally successful in counteracting antiwar isolationist climate preceding our involvement in the ongoing European conflict of WWI by engaging the Hollywood film industry to produce entertainment product favorable to the Allies. Creel recruited and motivated the biggest movie star performers of that era to participate in nationwide efforts to sell Victory Bonds. Both campaigns were highly significant in developing a climate of opinion that supported our eventual involvement in the war. To the isolationists and antiwar elements it was propaganda. To others it was a rallying cry to duty.

President Roosevelt found a similar quandary in the early years of Hitler's *Blitzkrieg* in Europe in the late 1930s and the early '40s.

When Hitler invaded Poland on September 1, 1939, and Great Britain declared war in Germany, American public opinion changed somewhat from earlier years. But in an early response to America's continued neutrality Congress passed a resolution that led to the forbidding in 1937 of the shipment of arms, ammunition, loans or credits to any belligerent, and carried a cash and carry provision for all nonmilitary supplies as well. Finally, in 1940, after the German conquests of France, the Netherlands, Belgium, and Norway, FDR was convinced that all-out aid must be given the Allies to protect the interest of the United States.

It was at this time that Roosevelt managed what is now considered an ingenious coup by his "Lend Lease" policy which allowed the transfer of 50 overaged destroyers to Great Britain in exchange for leases for naval bases on our Atlantic Coast from Newfoundland to British Guiana. Congress additionally passed a bill in the face of huge opposition in March 1941 that allowed the supply of all materials that would assist the Allies in the defeat of the Nazis. This amounted to a tacit declaration of war against the totalitarian powers and abandonment of neutrality.

Meantime, when Hitler took Paris in 1940, polls showed 64 percent of Americans were in favor of compulsory military training, and selective service was put into effect. The first drawing of men from ages 21 to 35 took place on October 29. This range of inductees was later extended to include men between 19 and 44 years old liable for call.

The Japanese attack on Pearl Harbor December 7, 1941, accelerated the call to arms of America's citizen soldiers.

General George Marshall, chairman of the Joint Chiefs of Staff, shared President Roosevelt's concern as to the morale of the newly drafted recruits into military service. He was determined that a widespread indoctrination effort be made in all armed forces branches to prepare them emotionally and mentally to adapt to their new and perhaps dangerous roles. He was further convinced that what was needed was not just a routine indoctrination product, but a dramatic depiction that would strike home to all of the new troops regardless of their intellectual level or their social economic backgrounds. Marshall knew of one man who he thought could produce motion pictures with these effective qualities. That unique individual was Frank Capra.

Chapter XIV

"The Directors"

FRANK CAPRA

Frank Capra was a director who demanded and got top billing on all of his motion pictures as *The Name above the Title*. He was a demanding negotiator with agents, studios and financiers alike, but once in production directed his actors with a light rein and a sure touch. He plowed through all obstacles in his path. He got things done, conventionally or otherwise. And he had the rare talent of depicting the American scene in such a way that he gained wide acceptance and popularity with the movie-going public and critics alike. "He was as American as apple pie," as the saying goes, though he was a foreign-born citizen of the United States.

Frank was five years old in 1903 when a letter came to Sicily, to the house of Salvatore Capra. A letter from a long lost oldest son, Frank's brother. Ben Capra had run away from home five years earlier and now wrote from an unheard of place in America: Los Angeles, California. The contents of the letter read to the gathered village by the local priest invited the family to join their son in America. No one in the Capra clan could read or write. Capra said his "later mania for education had its genesis in that letter"—and the fact that no one in his family could read it. The move to the new world was made and the Capras began a new life in Los Angeles. Young Frank worked at odd jobs through his entire schooling career, finishing high school in three and a half years, and graduating from Cal Tech with his degree in chemical engineering in June 1918. He promptly enlisted in the U.S. Army and was soon teaching ballistic mathematics to artillery officers at Fort Mason in San Francisco.

The Armistice came much to the relief of young Capra who was frustrated by the restrictions and controlled procedures enforced by the military. He found no opportunities for chemical engineers except those offered by the bootlegging industry then flourishing everywhere, but which he refused to support. Instead he "hit the road," and spent the next three years bumming around the western United States, hitching rides, riding the rails in boxcars, selling door to door, playing guitar in gin joints, living hand-to-mouth. He was down and nearly out. Finally his luck changed when he responded to an item in a San Francisco newspaper that announced the formation of a new movie studio, Fireside Productions. He "negotiated" a position with the new venture and was hired as a prop man.

He soon directed his first film; a one-reel silent movie based on a Kipling poem and called *The Ballad of Fultah Fisher's Boarding House*. This was the first of more than 60 films Capra would make over the next 25 years. Films that were made to entertain and on occasion to celebrate the human spirit.

* * * * *

Capra had never made a documentary film, but it occurred to him that the enemy had. Hitler's propaganda machine, conceived and managed by Goebbels, had produced hundreds of newsreel films and other products as had the Japanese. The director determined that the U.S. Department of Interior had a warehouse full of German and Japanese cinematic products of the last 20 years, and he conceived the idea of using selected cuts from these films to expose the enemy's true character and their evil designs. The transplanted movie director, now a major in the U.S. Army, managed to isolate his efforts from the more conventional military procedures of the Army Signal Corps, and gained a certain anonymity and unfettered authority in a subordinate unit, the 834th Photo Signal Detachment. He and a number of cronies he had recruited from his Hollywood stable produced seven 50-minute *Why We fight* indoctrination films as he had been ordered to do by General Marshall:

1. *Prelude To War* depicting Japan's conquest of Manchuria, and the invasion of Ethiopia by Mussolini

2. *The Nazi Strike.* The German advance into the Rheinland and Austria, the invasion of Poland, Czechoslovakia, and the initial phases of WWII

3. *Divide & Conquer.* Hitler's occupation of Denmark and Norway; the events at Dunkirk, and the occupation of France

4. *The Battle of Britain*

5. *The Battle of Russia, Moscow and Stalingrad*

6. *The Battle of China*

7. *War Comes To America*

These films were first designed for the indoctrination of U.S. Army troops and inductees, but were soon expanded for use as training films for the Navy, Marine Corps, and the Coast Guard. Soon it was distributed to the forces of the British, Canadian, Australian, and New Zealand military. The narrations and languages used in the films were translated into French, Spanish, Portuguese, and shown to our allies in China, South America and various parts of Europe and Asia. One film, *War Comes to America,* was released for widespread showing in American public theaters. All seven productions were shown to the British public upon order by Prime Minister Churchill. Russia also released the one showing the *Battle of Russia.*

Capra once remarked that he might be titled as the first *Voice of America.*

This effort probably represents "propaganda" at its best. If one thinks of the origin of the word, this too was propagation of the faith. The contents of these documentaries not only supported the morale of the troops to whom it was shown, but it created a wider mutual understanding with our Allies, and perhaps had a degree of intimidation to our enemies.

General Marshall was right. Major Frank Capra was the right man for this job.

* * * * *

JOHN HUSTON

When Capra arrived in Washington in 1942 he had been preceded by Darryl Zanuck, a recently recruited film expert and vice president of Twentieth Century Fox Studios, who was serving in the Army Signal Corps as a lieutenant colonel also supervising the production of training films. Capra and Zanuck, these two Hollywood luminaries, never actually worked together on projects, nor did either of them collaborate with yet another famed Hollywood director, John Huston, who had also been called to duty by the army in 1942.

Huston was a "very hot property" by Hollywood standards in the wake of his sensational success with a non-war film of 1941, *The Maltese Falcon*. Huston, commissioned a lieutenant by the army, was also attached to its Signal Corps and drew his first active duty assignment to produce a *Report from the Aleutians*. At this time enemy Japanese forces had occupied Attu and Kiska Islands, the tip of the Aleutian Chain in the North Pacific. His 47-minute documentary was highly regarded by the military, and its showing to civilian audiences drew rave notices from the *New York Times* and others.

Sporting the shoulder brass of a newly promoted captain, Huston was then sent to the Italian Campaign to cover the *Battle of San Pietro*. He entered the fray with the Texas regiment, the 143rd of the 36th Combat Division, and under fire produced an actual combat film, 32 minutes in length, that drew widespread praise from *Time* and the *Nation Magazine*. Promoted to major, he was awarded the Legion of Merit and released from active duty in 1945.

* * * * *

JOHN FORD

Rear Admiral J. Ford never commanded a U.S. Naval vessel, but he did fly enough combat missions off a flat top carrier during the Korean War in 1951 to be awarded an Air Medal. "The Admiral," John Feeney, Jr., was born in 1895 to Irish immigrant parents in Portland, Maine. As a young man he migrated to New York City to become an actor, and changed his name to John Ford. After a brief theatrical whirl he took Horace Greeley's advice and went west to California while his developing talent as a director of motion pictures was emerging. Within a few short years he became one of Tinsel Town's most prominent and successful directors.

During his long career he made 80 films, many considered classics, and discovered or developed screen stars John Wayne, Henry Fonda, Harry Carey, Victor McLaglen, Will Rogers, Maureen O'Hara, Ward Bond, and many others.

"Pappy," as he was called by his star actors and the technical people that accompanied him throughout his career, became famous for his depicting of the Old West (*Stagecoach*, and other movies), but what interested the military propagandists, particularly those in the navy, were early Ford films showing the U.S. Navy in action: *Salute, Men Without Women, The Sea Beneath,* and *Q-Ship.*

· The navy was appreciative of Ford's realistic depiction of the fleet in action, and John Ford, now familiar with life aboard navy ships while doing his commercial directorial duties, became more and more a dedicated navy man. He carried his enthusiasm over into his civilian life and created a yacht club with his cronies in the Hollywood Athletic Club, declared himself its commodore, and acquired a 110-foot ketch he named the *Alanar*. The "John Ford Navy" was formed.

The navy brass in the Los Angeles area was courted socially and professionally by Ford, and finally in September 1934, he was officially appointed a lieutenant commander in the U.S. Naval Reserve. With his new status as an actual naval officer, Ford recruited technicians from his commercial motion picture contacts and created a quasi-military group that became the Naval Field Photographic Unit, and staffed and equipped an operation that was later formally recognized by the navy when Ford was ordered to duty in September of 1941.

Ford's blockbuster wartime motion picture *Battle of Midway* was awarded an academy award Oscar for the best documentary of 1942. The director had been given leave to complete this most effective wartime motion picture, and in the wake of this success, and his performance record in North Africa he was requested by "Wild Bill" Donovan, head of the OSS (Office of Strategic Services), America's principal counterintelligence force, to produce a film depicting the Allied operations against the Japanese in Burma.

John Ford tackled the depiction of the Asiatic war in 1943 by going to film the C.B.I. (China, Burma, India) conflict with enthusiasm. He additionally functioned as a secret agent of the OSS in coordinating relations between General Claire Chenault, commanding general of the 14th Air Force, army commander Al Wedemeyer, and Lord Louis Mountbatten, the British chief. His purpose was to gain entry into the war zone by the OSS whose presence had been forbidden by Theater Commander Douglas MacArthur. Ford's dual efforts were successful; the OSS was established, and he completed *Victory in Burma,* which gained widespread praise in both the U.S. and England.

In 1944, OSS Chief Donovan did not forget the assistance afforded him by Naval Captain Ford in those earlier days in Burma, and he saw to it that Ford was given the appointment for the June 6, 1945, D-Day Invasion in Europe as the officer in charge of all Allied photographs.

Eighty hours of the only color film coverage of that historic D-Day event were finally released from government vaults for showing in 1999. President Harry Truman had refused Ford's request for a million dollar budget in 1945 to produce the film on the grounds the footage was too horrible for public consumption.

Upon his call to active duty, Ford's assignment was also the Army Signal Corps Pictorial Service. To give him greater freedom to produce combat films he was directed to organize field photographic camera crews to cover the invasion of North Africa in the summer of 1942. In addition to intelligence footage shot in the actual theatre of operations, he produced footage for a documentary titled *They Were Expendable.* The navy saw fit to reward him for his bravery under fire and his film productions by promoting him to captain, April 1944.

In 1950 the navy issued Ford's last combat assignment to produce a propaganda film about the current Korean conflict. He went to the theater in January 1951, met with General Douglas MacArthur and during the course of production flew enough air missions to win an Air Medal. Republic Pictures released *This is Korea* in 1951.

Wearing his Air Medal and Legion of Merit, and his new Star, newly promoted Rear Admiral John Ford was released from active duty in April 1945.

* * * * *

BILLY WILDER

The Allies at the end of WWII saw to the restoration of order in Europe and the punishment of those enemies who had committed crimes. Another movie director was called to serve his adopted country. Born in Austria of Jewish parents who died in Auschwitz during Hitler's reign of terror, Billy Wilder, one of Hollywood's all-time premier directors, was given the rank of colonel and ordered to Germany in 1954 to cover the Nuremberg Trials as a "propaganda analyst."

The United States Army has continued its long tradition of using the talents and technical abilities of the motion picture industry as recently as 1999 when it signed a 44.3 million dollar contract with the University of California to develop military combat simulations.

Army Secretary Louis Caldera said they wanted training programs "with very real story and character content to prepare them for missions they're going to do."

William Bond, commanding general of the Army's Simulation Training Instrumentation Command in Orlando, Florida, said: "We would like to make our training much more realistic. We want the ability to create a state where the soldier feels this is so real that he actually perspires, his heart rate goes up, and he reacts in a manner that is consistent with what he would do in a real environment."

These "Pentagonese" statements are reminiscent of the terse orders General George Marshall issued to Frank Capra in WWII. It's more than likely that modern director Steven Spielberg's sensationally realistic war epic, *Saving Private Ryan,* stimulated this most recent interest in a renewed collaboration between Hollywood and the military.

It would be appropriate to include Spielberg, Ford, Huston, Wilder, et al. on the list of those who demonstrated the effectiveness of motion pictures as perhaps the most effective device in directing human behavior.

Chapter XV

Ed Murrow

I was constantly intrigued by the commonalty of attitude exhibited by the variety of individuals I had to work with in the psywar branch. They came from various walks of life, with different academic interests, different inherent beliefs, and a wide expanse of economic and social environments. Yet they had a common attitude in the way they met the challenge thrust upon them by their involvement in psywar, and of course the Korean Conflict itself. There was no collegiate rah-rah for the team boys, but a serious mature approach to performing responsibly.

There was something sobering about our mission. There's no doubt that combat soldiers are well aware of the seriousness of training to kill or be killed by the enemy. That is indeed a *sobering* consideration. And actual combat is the ultimate test.

But psywar was a relatively new kind of combat. It is obvious that there was no chance of the psywarrior being a casualty. But we all were aware that what we did could result in the shortening of the war, reduce the loss of life of soldiers on each side of the conflict, and stop the killing of vast members of helpless civilians. The old adage about "the pen is mightier than the sword" had new significance. Those of us with perhaps a more idealistic bent even considered the possibility that we might in some way contribute to the hollow promise of WWI propagandists that this could be the *"War to end all Wars."*

All of this is not to imply that these young men did nothing else but spend all of their time peering into their individual crystal

99

balls. They were young, in their early twenties, most of them single, and well endowed with the desires and drives of healthy human beings. They played and pursued life with vigor, and some even acquired a taste for dry, straight up martinis. I made no attempt to control, direct, or organize their off-duty activities, though Donna and I did host regular social get-togethers. We were always delighted at the quality of the omelet served up by these young, brilliant egg heads.

Sunday afternoons were a time when we maintained a sort of ongoing open house. Our apartment in the Woodner on 16th Street had a fairly good-sized living room and our drop-in visitors varied from single bachelors to a few married couples. Donna acquired a collection of assorted overstuffed cushions and people sprawled all over the place. Entertainment presented no problem. Animated conversation prevailed, word games, and even that old party standby, charades. But the highlight of these occasions was the weekly appearance of Ed Murrow and his television report, "See It Now," on CBS that I could get on our 12-inch TV set.

"Hello America. This is London." Except for Winston Churchill, this had been the most familiar radio voice in the United Kingdom in WWII. I, and most of my mates in the 357th Fighter Group, Lieston, England, listened to this truly American voice whenever possible over the simulcast on the Armed Forces Radio Network. We'd huddle around our potbellied stoves with the incessant rain beating on the tin roofs of our Quonset huts and hear the uncensored on-the-scene report that Murrow delivered to our folks in the United States. We knew that they were getting it straight, and his word was as good as a letter home.

My first recollection of Ed Murrow was a CBS radio bulletin aired one afternoon in August 1940. It was nearly midnight in London and Murrow was witnessing the night bombing raid by the Nazi Luftwaffe that heralded the first blitz that became the Battle of Britain. As a journalism student this to me was news in its most dramatic form. This live, on-the-scene report surpassed what up until now had been the most sensational 1938 radio broadcast ever, the

Orson Welles make-believe realistic dramatization of H. G. Wells' *War of the Worlds*.

I had introduced Murrow's "Hear It Now" radio program to the radio propaganda class I had taught back at Gowen Field in Idaho. He had made his first trip to Korea in 1950, and his first broadcast had established him, as it had in WWII, as the most reliable voice reporting this war. My current group of psywar people had accepted Murrow then, and they now looked forward to his "See It Now" program with as much enthusiasm as I did.

There is little doubt that Murrow's broadcasts influenced public opinion and were extremely effective in bolstering not only the morale of the American audience but the British audience as well. The reasons for his successful impact offer useful criteria for creating radio propaganda that will be well received and achieve the desired results:

Content. His subject matter was first of all newsworthy. It concerned people from places that were familiar, and the nature of their plight stimulated sympathy for them and resentment toward their oppressor. There was no doubt as to the authenticity of the subject matter.

Style. Murrow's style was perhaps a *lack of style*. To the American ear there was little in his speech that reflected any region, ethnic origin, or literate level. He had no Yankee twang to offend the Southerner, or Midwest or Southwest drawl to grate on the New Yorker.

All radio network news executives for years had recruited their spokespersons from the Northwest: Oregon, Washington, and Idaho where provincial dialects were almost nonexistent. Murrow was born in North Carolina but was just past the age of five when his family moved to Blanchard, a farming and lumber community on Puget Sound, 70 miles north of Seattle, Washington. He went to work in the woods at the age of 14, so he knew the life of the common man. He graduated at Washington State College at Pullman in 1930. His background was all American and his voice and delivery reflected this heritage. As he matured he acquired a certain urbanity in attire as well as public manner that made him acceptable to all levels of society.

How do you find such a "voice" to deliver your radio propaganda missile? You can't, of course, find a Murrow. An obvious place to look is among the exiles in the West that are disaffected from their homelands by the Soviet expansion. For example, Padenewski, Poland's world famous pianist, composer, and prime minister of his country, was a very effective "voice" in WWI and again in 1940 when he became president of the Polish Parliament in Exile. Similar personages may be found from all of the countries behind the Iron Curtain to "sell" the message.

* * * * *

During the hiatus of 1953 when the negotiations were going on in Korea, the ARCS psywar branch devoted much of its off-duty time observing and analyzing the daily examples in the media of the molding of public opinion. Murrow and his team, resting on the laurels they had earned by their broadcasts during WWII, continued successfully in their coverage of political campaigns, and the current war. William Shiver authored a best seller. Eric Sevareid, also an author, was becoming a successful news analyst. The rest of the Murrow gang, Bob Trout, Bill Downs, Dick Hottelet, and Charles Collingwood, were all doing newscasts in a relatively unbiased objective manner in the Murrow style.

Individuals prominent in the printed media included Westbrook Pegler, Teddy White, Walter Lippmann, Drew Pearson, and many others who "covered," analyzed, and recorded political events, and of course the progress of the war in Korea.

ARCS's psywarriors were active in identifying the motivations of the various news people as to their private agendas: Republican, Democrat, liberal, conservative, antiwar "doves," and militant "hawks." Much of their coverage was biased, but we generally agreed that they mainly communicated with their own constituency and rarely changed the well-established attitudes of their opposition.

The electronic media presented another possibility to our analysts. The emotional impact on the radio and television audiences by the newscasters, commentators, and other analysts added a dimension that was absent from the printed word. In radio, the dulcet tones of the quietly persuasive baritone, or the strident harangue of the evangelical orator both caused a reaction appropriate to the goals of the speaker. Radio voices became as familiar and as trusted as those of members of one's own family. Television, as a device for creating an emotional rather than an intellectual reaction, was even more insidious in its impact. Though the written television script was objective in its content, a curled lip, a raised eyebrow, a bored stare could give the message a decidedly slanted meaning. Most television stars developed a *style* that distinguished them from their competitors, and gave them a unique quality that built a following for them, their sponsors, and their networks.

This subtle manipulation of news reporting to the general populace, information that many times was of vital importance to understanding national problems, was seen as a departure from the traditional methods used in *educating* the public.

Politicians using similar techniques in campaigning for election or debating issues as office holders always had a written record somewhere of their stated positions. If they proved to be liars or unfaithful to their promises they had the reckoning of their electorate who could vote them out of office, or in extreme cases, impeach them. Congress itself had committees and oversight capabilities that provided discipline to their members. No such devices existed for control of the media's behavior.

Not one member of my group disagreed with the protection provided by the First Amendment to the Bill of Rights guaranteeing freedom of the press. There was considerable agreement, however, that this *right* should rather be considered a *privilege* with certain responsibilities required of its practice.

Would it not be an idyllic solution if the entire body of journalists, written and spoken practitioners alike, would create a code of ethics and practices for their members, and establish a council that could enforce their compliance, perhaps not as a matter of law, but as an agreed procedure?

We were not optimistic about such a thing ever coming to pass. But it would be interesting to see which journalists supported the idea, and those that saw a violation of their cherished First Amendment.

Our group of young officers had become nearly as close-knit as men become when in a combat situation. Although almost each man held on somewhat to his earlier biases and prejudices related to politics, class affiliations, and regional attitudes, he nonetheless acquired a new broader posture in challenging all things that were now measured in how they influenced the general American public acceptance of information. Radio, newspapers, magazines, and now television all were scrutinized critically as to believability. Our group could not be called cynical but rather skeptical.

There was an abundance of daily public expression by the media to attract their attention. The recent national election campaigns were as usual a cornucopia of glittering generalities, half-truths, catch phrases, and buzz words designed to reach the emotions of the voters rather than appeals to reason and factual argument.

The "good news" policies of the military and the administration had deteriorated. President Truman's popularity when he left office was at an all-time low. President Eisenhower's election campaign promise to "Go to Korea," with the implication that it would soon be over, had not been realized as soon as the people hoped. The spring of 1953 was a continuance of a long period of frustration as the peace talks at Panmunjom went on and on.

The late winter and spring of 1952–53 was marked by Ed Murrow's remarkable *"Christmas in Korea"* broadcast, the death of Stalin and Senator Joseph McCarthy's witch-hunt attacks that even included a barrage aimed at The Voice of America. It was becoming almost impossible to determine psywar targets that were reusable themes for exploitation. My staff and crew could reasonably conclude that Harry Truman's "Police Action" was winding down, but we all realized a traditional victory for the United States was not in the cards. A line of demarcation at the 38th parallel between the U.N. forces and North Korea had first been suggested by the USSR's Jacob

Malik in July of 1950 and was finally agreed upon in November of 1952. Then came the negotiations for prisoner exchanges. The U.S. listed 143,000 military personnel and the North Koreans reduced the number to 11,500. The arguments went on and early this year of 1953 the exchange was finally made.

This was not a fertile environment for our brand of military operations. We presented a few projects that were designed to assist in postwar activities, principally with our U.N. allies, and the liberated South Koreans. But there was little that we could contribute that couldn't be better done by our State Department and through our seat in the United Nations. A fairly reliable rumor was afoot that the shelf life of the Air Force Psychological Warfare Division of ARCS was to be terminated, and our activities would be assigned to the National Security Council. We knew quite a lot about rumors and we were confident this was a believable one.

Chapter XVI

Miami Mission

"I need a few hours flying time this month," Colonel Swyter said, "to qualify for flight pay. You want to fly right seat in a B-25? Like over-night to Miami?" "Roger, Wilco," I said. "I'll get a pass from Donna."

Miami Beach was not Piccadilly Circus in WWII London, but Carl and I reverted to the old fighter jock mentality we had both enjoyed during those exciting wartime years. We did the town. I adroitly revived my taste for Scotch whiskey that I had acquired in England, but upgraded my booze budget to Johnny Walker *Black label* instead of the J.W. Red label, the less expensive blend that was available at that long ago time. Carl likewise adjusted his usual bar order and switched to Singapore Slings, a recipe for which he had to educate most of the bartenders we met.

Miami was great fun. We went "pub hopping." We had dinner at the Fountainbleu Hotel; then on to various night spots where we heard Jonnie Ray very briefly, then a couple of hours with the King Cole trio somewhere, and then the top of the evening with a favorite of mine, Myron Cohen, a great Jewish storyteller who knocked 'em dead. I haven't any idea what time we hit the sack.

Surprisingly, we both felt fine the next morning, and after a Bloody Mary and a great brunch, we hailed a cab about noon and headed for Homestead AFB where we had tied down the B-25 the day before.

The slight drizzle we'd noticed on the way out turned out to be a fringe indication of a line squall that was developing along our route back to Washington, D.C. Carl wasn't intimidated by the operations officer when we filed our flight plan, and though the Ops guy looked a little startled when Carl indicated a Visual Flight Regulation (VFR) he was not inclined to argue with a Bird Colonel wearing Command Pilot wings, and neither was I. I had assumed we'd file an Instrument Flight Regulation (IFR) plan considering the squalls, time of year, etc. But who was I to argue with a guy who had flown the "Hump" in some of the worst weather conditions in the world?

The line squalls developed into a small front, and the winds and rain soon acquired almost hurricane intensity as we progressed northward. We'd been in the air about an hour and were flying at altitudes less than five hundred feet; gusting winds from the East with increasing turbulence made this less than a casual trip home.

"That's Wilmington, North Carolina, ahead there on the left," Carl said. "I had a boat I kept there when I was stationed at Pope Air Force Base at Fayetteville a while back. Pope's about seventy some miles up the South River you see there. I know it pretty well and I think we'd better fly up that river and set this bird down for a spell."

Carl swung around the outskirts of Wilmington and we headed up that *Lazy River,* as the old song goes. He had his side window open where the visibility was better than the view through the solid mass of rain water that pelted our front windshield, and I knew at two hundred or so feet of altitude he could keep on course.

The colonel flew that old B-25 warhorse like we were on a strafing run. We had a quartering tail wind behind us and the turbulence was not too bad. I soon was able to make an identifying call to our destination: "Pope Tower. Pope Tower. This is Air Force 7348. VFR from Homestead Air Force Base. We are a B-25 approximately 30 miles southeast of your station. Request permission to land and request landing instructions. Over."

A response from Pope was loud and clear: "Air Force 7348. This is Pope Tower. You are cleared to land, runway niner zero. We have no traffic, heavy rain, wind at 40 miles per hour, steady from 90 degrees. Barometer at 29.62. Over."

I responded: "Roger, Pope Tower. Our landing pattern may be a little unconventional. We will call on final. Out."

I looked at Carl in the left first pilot seat. He nodded indicating he'd heard the transmissions.

Colonel Swyter was a command pilot and had logged a couple of thousand miles or more flying time in probably a dozen different aircraft. He had begun his flying career as a pursuit pilot in Hawaii with now-General Norstadt in the 1930s when they were both second lieutenants. WWII found him flying the "Hump" over the Himalayas in the China Burma India theater. And he could fly this B-25 like he'd invented it. To say that I was glad he was flying this airplane would be a massive understatement.

Carl hollered at me over the engine noise coming through the open window, "Fayetteville dead ahead. Call Pope. We're 15 miles out on a heading of 320 approaching to land on runway niner zero." I quickly complied and Pope Tower confirmed.

My pilot called for half flaps, slowed the air speed down and then to lower landing gear. And there it was . . . Pope air strip, well lighted.

Carl called for full flaps and turned to 270, our "down wind" leg for landing. Two more really good descending left turns and we were on final approach, Carl still looking out the window though we could see the blurred runway lights through the flooded windshield.

First pilot Swyter greased it in. I was not surprised. We taxied behind the FOLLOW ME jeep waiting at the intersection and followed it to a hardstand in front of the central tower. We closed our bird down, disembarked, and then ran 20 or so feet from the belly of the B-25 to a waiting staff car. As we pulled away I noticed a ground crew tying down the plane in what was now a full-blown storm with horizontal sheets of rain driven by a strong wind. An airman held an umbrella for the colonel when we got to operations. I got wet.

The early morning trip back to Washington was uneventful, clear skies all the way. The B-25 seemed to purr all the way back in contrast to the deafening racket I had shuddered at when we first fired

A Mitchell bomber, B-25J

her up. I must have gotten accustomed to those two Wright Cyclone 1750 horsepower engines the night before in the storm when the noise was a welcome reassurance that this mighty bomber could handle a lot worse.

My command pilot and I parted company in the parking lot outside Operations at Andrews after checking in. The time was 0805 and obviously we were going to be late for work. "Don't worry about it, Ab," Carl said. "I'll take care of it."

* * * * *

Colonel Carl Swyter couldn't "take care of it." I arrived at ARCS headquarters at 0930 after a brief stop at our apartment for a quick shower and a change of uniform. I decided to report in with the OD (Officer of the Day), explain my tardiness, and join up with my staff. They applauded when I walked in.

"Thank God you're alive, Sir," Bill Blatty deadpanned. "We were afraid you might have been shot down over Miami." "It's great to have you back, Sir," Lieutenant Rublee joined in with a wicked grin. "We were concerned you might be replaced with a Yale man." This broke up the rest of the grinning crew and they reluctantly wandered back to their desks still chuckling and obviously very pleased with their performance.

The rest of the day passed in a routine manner until just before 1700 hours a messenger arrived from the command's Exec office and dropped a bomb on my desk.

An RBI in the military is not a baseball term for "Runs Batted In." It's an order from a superior to "Reply by Endorsement" explaining an infraction of a regulation or a behavior deemed to be unacceptable to the commanding officer. This RBI was signed by the CO, General Monroe McCloskey.

I must admit I was stunned. During my military career I had received a few medals, awards, and decorations, but never an RBI! This piece of paper represented the very opposite of anything that had ever happened to me. I couldn't believe my eyes.

A kaleidoscope of questions raced through my mind. What in hell is this? I was the copilot of a flight commanded by a full colonel who was in complete charge of the whole operation. How could I be responsible for anything? Wasn't protecting government property by landing the aircraft in hurricane conditions a valid decision? Didn't we have proper clearances and approval for a cross country overnight training flight? Migod, they're done every weekend by all flying personnel in the organization to maintain their flying status and proficiency and to qualify for flying pay. Was being late for work for the first time in my career at ARCS an infraction that called for this? "What in hell is this?" I said to myself for the umpteenth time.

Finally, it occurred to me that the RBI probably killed any chance I had for promotion. Strangely enough, this fact didn't have as much weight as the knowledge that I now had a blemish, no matter the outcome, on my personal 201 military history file. Colonel Swyter had assured me on several occasions that I was a cinch for promotion to major. I had a few superior efficiency ratings, I had time enough in grade, and I held a position calling for a higher rank. He said the promotion board was made up of colonels and he knew some of them. I had it made!

I did as ordered and replied by endorsement. I'm afraid I did not compose my response in a contrite manner. I explained, I described the circumstances, I did not apologize, and I argued. I requested that the RBI be withdrawn and not be made a part of my record. That was the last correspondence I had on the matter. When the promotion list came out some weeks later, I was not on it. It's possible the military knew me better than I did.

* * * * *

It was this time in the late spring of '53, that I began to have second thoughts about seeking a military career in a peacetime environment. I must admit, the prospect of being promoted to major, to field grade, had held considerable attraction. And now that the promotion would not be just delayed, but maybe eighty-sixed for good if that RBI hovered on my record, a future in the air force looked pretty dim. Strangely enough I was not as disappointed as I would have expected. My combat tour in England in WWII, and even this present assignment in psywar, though it was not an active operational mission, had been an experience I would treasure forever. But I was becoming more and more aware of the *politics* that seemed to be an integral part of successful progress up the career ladder in the peace time military establishment. Finding a sponsor, a ranking superior that would advance your progress with good efficiency ratings, and promotions, was essential. You had to be meritorious in your performance, of course, and also agile in your ability to gain the support of your subordinates. But more importantly, to get along with your superiors. The GIs had a name for it: "Brown-nosing." I was never very good at it.

I do not intend to be too critical of the system. Recent history strongly indicates the need for high-ranking generals to be extremely competent in the political area. The ability to work effectively with the War Department, the Defense Department, Congress oversight committees, or the heads of state is fundamental. Our current president, Eisenhower, had all of the necessary attributes to not only direct the performance of the generals under him that he had leap-frogged with his promotions by President Roosevelt, but to deal successfully with Churchill, deGaulle, and Truman. No, the system is undoubtedly correct, and I have great respect for those career officers who dedicate their lives to this form of public service.

But, I was becoming more and more convinced that this life was not for me. As a reserve officer rather than regular army I knew that I was ill-equipped to compete with War College graduates, and though I'd miss the camaraderie of life that existed in the service, I'd better wait for another war. This one was winding down. Ike had said he'd "go to Korea," and I thought I'd better go back to Oregon when it was over.

Chapter XVII

"Over and Out"

"Andrews tower. This is B6R, F-51, fifteen miles south of your station requesting permission to make a straight in approach and landing."

"Roger, B6R, this is Andrews. You are cleared to land, runway 36, winds are calm."

I let down from altitude over Chesapeake Bay south of the District, and took up a heading for the field to the north. I descended to about 50 feet from the deck and swept over the fairly level terrain at about 200 mph indicated air speed. As I crossed the end of the runway I pulled up sharply, killing my speed in a leaning loop to the left, cut power and dropped wheels at the top. Maintaining the now diving turn, I lowered 15 degrees of flaps as I turned in line with the runway. I touched down making a wheel landing, completing the tactical landing maneuver.

The voice from the control tower sounded slightly amused.

"That's a nice landing, Captain Abner, but at Andrews we have a 300-foot altitude, rectangular landing pattern."

"Roger Andrews," I replied. "Sorry, Andrews, next time for sure." That was my first flight out of Andrews.

The air force had recalled me to active service at my reserve officer rank on flying status as a single-engine pilot. This last item was an important addition as it allowed me to fly copilot in multi-engine aircraft, solo in single-engine fighters, AT-6s and to qualify for a monthly flying pay allowance requiring only four hours flying time each month.

Daisy Mae, my combat Mustang P-51

I had earned my flying pay at McChord AFB in the right seat of C-47s, C-45s, C-54s, and Mountain Home AFB in Idaho in C-47s, and an occasional solo hop in a busy AT-6 trainer. I was delighted when I arrived for duty in Washington, D.C., to learn that nearby Andrews AFB had a half dozen F-51 Mustangs that were air worthy and rather neglected, as few pilots in the area checked them out. The crew chiefs of these sitting birds were always delighted to see me, and they got a big kick out of my combat style tactical landing approach on my first local mission.

My schedule at Georgetown and now at ARCS Headquarters still accommodated my being able to schedule two or three flights a month in my old war-horse, the Mustang. But today, I had the feeling this would be my last flight in this mount that had served me so well for so long.

This day I wandered around out of traffic at a safe altitude, staying generally in the local flying area, not wanting to file a flight plan for a triangular cross country training flight as I had done in the past.

I had wandered aimlessly off shore over the Atlantic Ocean, scanning the beaches and villages along the shoreline. The weather was fairly good with a few small cumulus formations here and there, and it was with some surprise that I found myself in sight of New York City.

I was so taken with the awesome sight of those towering skyscrapers, some lighted as the late afternoon was turning into dusk, that I increased my altitude to 10,000 feet and made a wide circle around the city.

I had seen many European cities from the air during WWII: London, Paris, Berlin, Munich, etc., all gray and ominous from the bombings by the Nazis and of course by our Allied efforts. This almost surrealistic scene of our Big Apple seemed somehow a symbolic final finish to my waning career as a fighter-pilot. It was a very emotional moment for me, and I was somewhat hypnotized by this unusual experience. I was still in a rather detached frame of mind as I completed my circuit of the now darkening city and automatically took up a heading back to my home base at Andrews.

I was suddenly shaken back to reality when I became aware of an F-80 jet fighter some one hundred feet off my left wing, and another flanking me on the right. I could clearly see the pilot on my left talking to someone, apparently getting an identification of me from his ground control. These two interceptors were obviously from the Air Defense Command, and I obviously was in a restricted area.

I waggled my wings slightly in what I hoped was a friendly manner, and slapped myself in the head as if to say I was stupid but friendly.

They escorted me for perhaps five minutes, then with a slight waggle of wings, they peeled off and were gone.

As I pulled up and swung into my hardstand back on the ground at Andrews, I looked around half expecting a reception committee consisting of the Officer of the Day, an A.P. or two, and a dark blue command car that would transport me to Base Operations en route to the brig. But only the crew chief greeted me, and when he'd finished placing chocks and tying down my faithful steed, probably for the last time for me, he drove me in a jeep to the parking lot where my convertible was parked.

I had arrived just in time to put up the car's top as the darkening mist was turning into a drizzle and promising a more sincere rain. As I proceeded down the crowded parkway back to the District, my earlier mood had been replaced by a rather resigned attitude.

"I wonder if I've now achieved my first flying infraction? Maybe another RBI to dress up my 201 file. To hell with it. That flight over the Big City was worth it. C'est la Guerre!"

Off We Go . . . .

Epilogue

Looking back, we see a war that wasn't won, and a fragile peace that became a sort of witch's brew that fermented for more than four decades, always threatening to boil over. The Cold War ended with the collapse of the Soviet Union and the international appeal of communism theories in shambles, and the only remnants remaining are those isolated cells of communist satellites that maintain the Red label but are, in fact, relatively petty dictatorships whose threats rely on modern weapons of destruction and acts of terrorism.

Conflicts between armies are rare, but the war of words continues, accompanied by acts of violence, subversion, and intimidation. Even the political scene in benevolent societies has been sullied by the covert campaigns waged by the "Spin Doctors" whose products are eagerly accepted by a voracious, sensationally oriented press.

Psywar, in its worst form, is alive and kicking. Propaganda in spite of its early Christian origins is again a dirty word.